How to Change Your Life for the Better

by

JOSEPH J. FOSTER, III
and
T. L. FOSTER

International Standard Book Number
0-931494-69-9

Library of Congress Card Catalog Number
85-70676

First Original Edition

Published in the United States of America

by

BRUNSWICK PUBLISHING COMPANY
LAWRENCEVILLE, VIRGINIA 23868

CONTENTS

INTRODUCTION

This book has been prepared to include as much about self-help as is possible. Many books of this type are limited in their information. Even if you read many of them, you might not get all of the information that is in this book. To me some titles are more of one chapter material than a full-length book, but somehow some authors get a book out of one chapter. The book on positive thinking is a whole book on one subject where as this one only uses one chapter on it. There are many subjects in this book and it's as it should be, in my opinion. A book on one subject is good, but if one covers a wider range of subjects it may be better. Instead of five books you only have to read one to get a lot of information on a variety of subjects.

This book was written with the idea that it would be a complete guide to a new life for you, the reader. If you only replace one bad habit with one good habit as a result of reading the book, then it's been a success for you. The more changes for the better that you make the better it is for you. After you've read the book you can keep it handy for reference. It would be a good idea to read it over several times so that you become completely familiar with its contents.

Chapter 1

AS YE SOW...

All of the good self-help books talk in general terms. These generalizations can be applied to everyday life on a specific basis. I once argued this point fruitlessly with a friend. In order to have the best of both worlds, I am going to write the first chapter like other authors before me. The later chapters will be more specific.

You can find a great deal of help in the Bible. The title of this chapter is found in the Bible: "As ye sow so shall ye reap." This is one of the basic principles of self-help. Whatever you do in life it is returned to you. How many times have you seen a movie where the husband cheats on his wife only to find that she had just cheated on him? Well that's the way it works. If you do bad things you get bad things in return, and if you do good things you get good things in return. Life has a way of evening the score. It may take some time to get what you have coming, but get it you will. A friend of mine was in his garage one day in California and he had a long electric extension cable he had gotten from his brother. I asked him about it and he said that his brother had stolen it from a construction job where he worked. Later in the conversation he told me that his brother had just gotten a traffic ticket. I drew a comparison for him of how his brother had stolen a $25.00 cable and life made him pay a $25.00 traffic ticket. He was now even on that account by life's standards. It wasn't fair to the construction company, but the brother had gained nothing. He sowed and he reaped. It's the same for everyone. You probably can think of a similar example in your life. It doesn't have to be a negative example. It can be something good.

Another friend of mine told me about his girlfriend and what happened to him and right away I spotted life's justice in his life. He was a married man with a girlfriend on the side. He was willing to leave his wife for this girl. One day she told him that she was pregnant and he was happy and told her now we can get married. He was surprised when she told him that the baby wasn't his. That ended their relationship. His wife was hurt by his fooling around and he was hurt from the very girl he was in love with. He sowed and he reaped. If you're religious you could say there's a big bookkeeper in the sky who keeps a record of all the good you do and all the bad, and sooner or later he evens the score in your life. It works in a strange way. If you do something bad to one person you would think that the revenge would have to come from that person. It's the logical thing to think but it isn't so. It can come from anywhere. Another friend cheated on his wife and finally felt guilty about it so he told her and asked forgiveness. She said she'd try, but in time wound up cheating on him. He found out about her and tried to forgive her but he couldn't any more than she could forgive him and their marriage broke up. Another friend put it in his own terms: "What goes around comes around." It's a law of nature that never fails. You should know about it and beware that it does not bring bad things into your life. You can use this law to your advantage. So far I've only given bad examples but it works in reverse as well. I once bought a man Christmas dinner at a diner where I was eating. I felt that he had no money to buy his own as he only ordered coffee. I offered to buy his meal and he accepted. Later in the day I found a twenty-dollar bill. I had been overpaid for my kindness. This will happen sometimes. An over-payment for a deed will occur.

If a lot of negative things are happening in your life you need to take stock of your habits. You may have to do some changing in your life. It could be that you're doing the wrong things and reaping the benefits of your actions. The rewards don't always make sense. You have to interpret what is going on in your life. Maybe you're a mother and you're always hollering at your kids sometimes more than they deserve. All of a sudden the roof leaks and it's a nuisance. Well don't you think that hollering at your kids is a nuisance to them. It works at any age level. Let's say your child is a bully. He goes around roughing up the smaller kids. One day he goes swimming and bursts his head open by accident. He had it coming. It isn't likely that he could figure out the scheme. The sooner a person, finds out about this law, the better they will be. I'm sure you've heard of comeuppance. It's the same thing, but it applies to all ages. You may have heard someone say "One of these days he'll get his comeuppance." This isn't said much these days but it was years ago. The principle has been around a long time. It's good to know about. You can start today by trying to do only good things and sit back and wait for the rewards to come in. You're on the right track already by reading this book. You can get other books on the same subject. If you're short on cash you could make a trip to the nearby library and read for free. I hope that after reading this book you'll have a good understanding of how to make your life a better one and not need to read any other books. Sometimes one author doesn't get his point across as well as another for you. People are different and their learning habits are different too. Even if you understand everything in this book it would be a good idea to read others as well. I've read books by Norman Vincent Peale, Earl Nightingale and W. Clement Stone to mention a few of the best. I met W. Clement Stone at a seminar. These are truly great men and you should read their material. You can get a different point of view or the same thing put another way may give you a better understanding of the matter. These men are all wealthy and they got that way by using certain principles. You can do the same thing. The key to any success is to do your homework first. You've got to learn the right principles and then apply them to attain riches. This is true of all riches whether they be material or spiritual. This chapter deals with one of the basic principles. As ye sow...It's never too late and you're never too old to change your life for the better. Some people make the change late in life and are only sorry that they didn't do it sooner so that they could have enjoyed the good things for a longer period of time. Since we can't turn back the clock we have to start where we are now. This book can be the beginning of a great new life for you. Did you ever get an unexpected check in the mail or an unexpected inheritance. You must have done something right. You see the principle works even if you don't know about it. Knowing about it just makes it easier to do something about it and make your life better by taking deliberate action. You may think that you're not going to do anything with this new knowledge, but you will. You have to go through life doing one thing or another. Maybe you'll free a dog from a fence or help a cat from a tree. This will be rewarded sometime in your life. You may kick the dog or leave the cat in the tree. You'll get the benefits from those actions as well but the results won't be good. As I have said you get out of life what you put into it. Good comes from good and bad comes from bad. It's like using the right ingredients when you cook something. If you use the right ingredients you will get a good result and if you use the wrong ingredients you will get a bad result. You wouldn't put onions in a cake mix. This would be a bad ingredient to use. It follows then that you shouldn't do bad things as you go through life. Not now since you know that you will get bad things in return for the bad you do. The world would be a better place if everyone knew this principle and practiced it everyday in their lives. You can do your part by doing good in your life. The people around you will take a different look at you and you'll like your new image. You will feel good about yourself. You could start today. You could read a chapter and put it into practice and when you have it down pat you could read another chapter and put it into practice and so on until you finish the book. If you read straight through you can come back and refresh your memory. They say that you don't really learn a thing until you've reviewed it five times. Don't be afraid to read it over and over again. Learn this material and start a better life today. Once again "As ye sow so shall ye reap." It's in the Bible. There are lots of good things in the Bible to learn and make your life a better one. Bible tapes are sold now so that you can listen effortlessly to the New Testament. If reading is a chore, try the tapes. In fact the Bible is one of the best self-help books ever written. There is much wisdom in the Bible. I strongly suggest that you make it "must-reading." It wouldn't hurt to read it in it's entirety but you could concentrate on the New Testament to cut down on the material. Jesus did no harm to any man and it would be a good idea to fashion your life after his in as much as you can. Of course you won't go around working miracles every day, but you could refrain from doing anyone harm. Try this new idea in your life for thirty days and see if you don't feel much better about yourself. It's amazing how this one little thing can change your life for the better. You now know about one of the strongest laws in existence. It's up to you to decide on how you are going to use it. It can be used for good or evil purposes. Just remember that you will reap the benefits whether they are good or bad. Like most people I've had some good and some bad in my life. Sometimes the things that happen happen out of the blue and there seems to be no explanation for them. Recently I was at the dog track and had made my bet and was going outside to watch the race. In the midst of the crowd I spotted something on the floor near the door. Anyone could have seen it but I was the lucky soul to find a hundred dollar bill lying there among all of the people. I couldn't believe it. Why hadn't someone else found it? There were plenty of people nearby but I made a clean find and was able to pick up the bill without racing with someone else. The only logical reason for this good luck had to be a reward for a previous deed. I didn't know what I was being rewarded for but was happy to find the money. You may have similar luck at a bingo game and win time after time or win a lot in one game. It could be that you get lucky on one of the lotteries. Maybe a contest or giveaway will smile on you. There are all kinds of ways to get your rewards or punishments. You may have played a trick on a friend when you were young and the law of evens is just now getting around to get even with you for a nasty trick years ago. The car breaks down and on top of it all it's raining. There's no rhyme or reason to the law of evens. It takes its toll or gives its rewards in the strangest ways. If you're aware of this you can do something about it and change your life for the better.

There are some things in life that seem to have no reason at all or seem too severe for a small crime against nature. I surmise that God had a reason for these afflictions. It could have been the law of evens or it could be for a reason known only to God. There are some mysteries in life. We want to know all we can about little-known-laws and put them to our best uses. The mysteries will have to remain mysteries. We want to deal with the facts that we can learn and put to practical use in our daily lives.

You may have heard someone say "That's my Karma." Karma is another way of expressing the "Law of Evens." People refer to Karma as if it were fate or destiny. Almost as if it were predestined. This is a mistake. It's another mystery of how we can have a fate and at the same time choose our own fate. It's true; our lives are predestined, but at the same time we can choose our destiny. The main thing to remember is that we have the choice of how our lives can be. This phenomenon can be called Karma or the "Law of Evens" or you can say as ye sow so shall ye reap. It's the same thing. The two things that I want you to learn from this chapter are: #1 You have a choice; #2 You get back from life what you put into it. Those two points are the whole basis of this chapter. You can use this knowledge in your everyday life to make it better. Minimize the bad things that you do and maximize the good things and your life will be a better one.

It would be a good idea to make two lists of your habits and begin eliminating the bad ones. The list of good habits will give you confidence. Don't worry if the bad ones are more than the good ones. You are going to start eliminating the bad ones so that the list of good ones is the bigger list in as short of a time as possible. Think over your habits carefully and don't cheat on your lists. You would only be cheating yourself. To make it work you have to be honest with yourself. To simplify the task of changing the bad ones you could take one a week from the top of the list and concentrate on only one bad habit. If you eliminate it in a week's time, then take the next one and begin work on it. If you don't eliminate the first one in one week, then try to do it the next week. Work on each one until you've mastered it. When you've finished the list you could make another list and replace all of the bad habits with good ones. If you had ten bad ones then make a list of ten good ones and staɪ with the first one until it becomes a part of your life. This is a good idea for obvious reasons. The more good things that you do the better are your chances for more rewards. Not only will more good things happen to you, but fewer bad things will happen in your life. Wouldn't that be nice for a change? Take a little time to think of some of the things that could happen in your life and how nice it would be to do without a flat tire or broken grocery bag. I don't guarantee that your life will be all roses, but the more good habits you have, the better are your chances to have more good things happen in your life and less bad things. The sooner you get started, the better. I suggest

that after you read this chapter you put the book down until
you've made your lists and have begun to eliminate the
negative habits from your life. Once you have started this you
can begin reading again. Be thorough when you make your lists
and be honest with yourself. You have everything to gain.

Chapter 2

PAINT A PICTURE

A long time ago I developed an idea that you or me or anyone for that matter could paint a picture and then become that picture. I had read a lot of self-help books by that time. The message was clear. If you didn't like the person you were, you could change to another person. It's all in the way you think. If you think you're a failure, then you're a failure. If you think you're a success, then you're a success. A book I read pointed this out with the following statement." "Father was never a success because Father never made up his mind to be a success." That's the whole idea of it in a nutshell. You have to make the decision to be something else. Of course there's more to it than that. You don't decide to be a brain surgeon one day and then the next day you are one. That would be like telling the fireplace to give you heat when you hadn't put in the wood for the fire. You can be anything that you set out to be if you pay the price. No matter, what it is, you have to pay the price. Once you've done this your goal can be yours. Dare to think big. Set realistic goals for yourself. You can get burned out with all this information if you set your goals too high and fail to reach them. Be realistic. Realize that becoming that new person isn't going to be the easiest thing you ever did. It will take work on your part and it will be worth it in the end.

Let's say you're part of a working family and your income is needed to get by. Further let's say that you're good with hair. You might consider a course in cosmetology or one for a barber. You could go about this in two ways. You could work full-time and take courses part time or visa versa. This is just one example that has a sound basis. The new you probably doesn't know anything about the new line of work and knowledge of your new field is a must. Failure occurs from lack of knowlege. You must have knowledge and or practical experience. Using the above example you may think you're going to be content when you finish with your training and you may be, but if you want wealth you're going to have to do better than working for the other guy. He's the one making all of the money. Once you've mastered the trade you'll want to own your own shop and have others working for you. In the cosmetology business you could have your employees working on a 50/50 basis. Half of the money that they take in would be yours. If you had six employees you'd have the money of four people. That is if you worked in the shop yourself. You'd have all of the money and half of six others or three full salaries plus yours. From this you would have to pay the expenses but you would still be better off than working for someone else. You may be timid and think, "Oh! I couldn't do that." I mentioned before dare to think big. You could do that if you tried hard enough. Other people are doing it everyday. Why not you?

When you're making these changes in your life try to stay away from the wrong kind of people. Many people are jealous of you and your accomplishments. They will say things like "You couldn't do that" or "You're not good enough to do it," or "You don't have the brains to do it." If you listen to these people you are going to be defeated before you get started. Usually the members of your family will give you encouragement and this will help you to attain your goal. Your family is happy to see you succeed, but others are jealous and it would make them feel inferior if you made something out of your life. They are comfortable with you the way you are. Your success makes you better than they are and they wouldn't like that one bit. Don't be influenced by negative people. Be around people who will give you encouragement. This will help you win the battle.

It would be a good idea to find out what you're best suited for and you should choose one of these fields for a new line of work. If there's no way you can be an owner in this new field you want a good salary. If your salary gives you excess cash you can invest it and get a nice piece of the pie in that way. If you're going to get ahead, really ahead, you'll need more going for you than just the average job. If you have a job that puts you in the middle class you'll likely never get wealthy or independent, let alone rich. You need something more than just a job in most cases. We'll go into deeper detail in a later chapter.

There are other aspects of your overall picture. Personality is another thing you will want to consider. Getting along well with others is a must. If you don't get along well with others you will have to work on this phase of your personality. Make a list of your good points and your bad ones. Just like before take one thing at a time and eliminate the bad ones one at a time. When you've done this replace the bad ones with new good ones. Deal with how you get along with others. You should have a pleasant relationship with everyone you come in contact with.Your family relationship is especially important. Losing your temper or getting mad is a bad trait. It should be eliminated. You can win an argument and lose a friend. Don't argue with people; it doesn't pay in the long run. 'I'm not saying that you shouldn't stand up for your rights because you should but only to a point. If a mistake is made in a restaurant you should have it corrected whether it's the food or the price. There's a time to stand up for your rights and discuss the matter calmly. Don't be a jerk. You don't have to to get the job done.

Another thing is attitude. A positive mental attitude will take you far in life. It's essential to success. You attitude is the most important thing in your life. Always have a positive attitude.

Attitude will do more for you than you know. If you set a goal with a poor attitude you probably will not reach it. However, if you set a goal with a good attitude you have a good chance of reaching it. It's mental attitude that leads to success more than any other thing. In order to paint a picture and then become that picture you will need a positive mental attitude on your side. Don't be too general as this leads to failure. Don't set your goals too high as this leads to failure too. When you're trying to become success-conscious you will do better when you succeed a little at a time. One little success will give you encouragement to try another task with hopes of success of it. These little successes build your confidence. This is a big help in your quest to become the new picture that you've painted. Becoming the new picture can be easy. It's like using building blocks to make a pyramid. You do it one block at a time. The bottom blocks are the easiest. That's how it should be with the goals you need to accomplish to be the new picture that you've painted for yourself. Make a list of your goals in any order. Next ponder the list and determine the easiest goal on the list and then the next one and so on until the new list has the easiest goal on the top and the hardest one on the bottom. Now you can start at the top of the list and work your way to the bottom. When you've finished the list you will be the new person that you set out to be in the first place. Since nobody's perfect you will want to work on bad habits and bad personality traits as well as the other things that are important to you. Material things will probably require more money so you will want to consider ways to increase your income to get those material things. You could use a new car or a new place to live. Instead of renting you may want to buy a place of your own. Good counseling would be useful but if it's too expensive for you, you can find help in books. You may be surprised what you can find in a book!

While you're working on reaching your goals and especially

your main goal or a complete new you, it will be helpful to visualize this new you in your own mind. It's a good idea to spend one hour a day by yourself thinking about the new you. This one-hour thinking process will be a great help in accomplishing your goals. See it in your mind and believe it will happen and it will if you put forth the effort needed. You don't want to be a dreamer and dream your life away. It's good to have a dream, but you have to act on that dream to make it come true for you. A dream is useless without action. You've got to act on this vision to make it come true. Don't be lazy. Put out the effort needed to be a success. People with less education than you have done it and so can you. I've read story after story about millionaires who don't have a formal education and make it big in this country. One man was paralyzed and basically only had a sound mind to work with and put his family to work for him as well, and they made millions off of his ideas. Here's a man bedridden who made millions. If it's that easy for him it should be twice as easy for you and me with all of our facilities. If you happen to be limited in some way just think of the example and have courage. You, too, can succeed in life!

Another man bargained with Coca Cola and got a large sum of money for an envelope. When the people of Coca Cola had paid him and opened the envelopes they found a note that said "bottle it". Coke had gotten their money's worth and the man who had the idea had a nice profit.

I've found that I've got a talent for writing. I took college courses in English literature and composition and always made good marks in English. I enjoy it and it's profitable. If you can do the same that's good. If not, there's a niche for you to fit in where you can make out O.K.

You will find that the two main money-makers are either products or services. If you work for the other guy you render a service. You can render a service through you own business. On the other hand you could sell a product. There are some variations to these two main ideas. You could buy real estate to resell it at a profit. There are many ways to turn a profit. You will have to find one that works for you. You may go from one thing to another in your search for your right spot. Don't feel badly about it and don't let anyone convince you that you are a bum or wishy washy because you have to move around. Executives do it all of the time. It's all right to stay in one place for thirty years if it's right for you. On the other hand if it's not the right place for you, don't hesitate to change. It would be a sad state of affairs if you were stuck in a dead-end spot for your entire life. Don't think that you owe anybody anything. Look out for yourself. Well placed loyalty is a fine thing, but the company may give you a bad deal in the end. All too many times a person works for the other guy and doesn't make out well in the end. I know a couple who both worked in a shoe factory for fifteen years and twelve years and when the factory closed the union had to fight for their pension of $29.00 per month. This happened in the 1970's. It wasn't back at the turn of the century when $29.00 would buy something. Twenty-nine dollars ($29.00) was the total for both of them. There are many other examples of people getting bad deals from companies where they have worked a lifetime. Working for the other guy can be a necessary evil, but you have to get away from that kind of situation as soon as possible. The exception to this is if you are making enough to have an excess of cash to invest in something else. If you can live on $5.00 per hour and you're making $10.00 per hour you can stay on a while.

Chapter 3

PRAYER

Another big part of your life should be prayer. It doesn't matter what religion you are. Prayer is universal. It works for everyone. You may not always get what you want in the time period that you want it in, but prayer does work. It's another one of life's mysteries. Sometimes you may think it's useless but then one little prayer will be answered and your faith will be renewed. You should set aside thirty to sixty minutes a day for prayer. This may mean that you have to get up earlier or watch less T.V., but it's not too hard to do and you will feel better by doing it. I strongly recommend that before you end any of your prayer sessions you give thanks to God for your blessings. You can ask Him for help or just talk things over with Him. Sometimes you may draw a blank and not know what to say. This can happen when you visit with God everyday. Don't worry about it. He will know that you spent the time with Him and will appreciate it.

It may very well be the prayers of thousands that give us world peace. There is a group called the Rosicrucians who use group prayer for good things in our world. Every month in their magazine they pick a subject to direct their prayers toward. Then at a specific time on a specific day all of the members say a prayer for that goal. I think that this is a fine thing. I know when I am anxious for some good thing to happen in my life I ask the aid of others to say prayers for me and when they come to be I give thanks to the Lord. I've heard that it's not proper to ask for money but I think that if you do it in an indirect way it's acceptable. You could pray that you reach all of your goals and one of them could be to have a lot of money by time you're 35 or some other specific age. Thirty-five is long gone for me and I'm not a millionaire yet but I'm not giving up. Whatever stage you are now you can always go higher. Let's say that you are an atheist and don't believe in God. What has prayer got to offer you? Well, if you ponder the question is there a God you can only get two possible answers: yes or no. If it's no then you would be wasting your time by praying, but if it's yes you could reap great rewards that might not be possible otherwise. Wasting your time isn't the best thing you could do but just for the sake of argument why not try prayer for less than thirty minutes a day. Just wishing for good things to happen is a form of prayer and no doubt you've wished for something at one time or another. Try doing it as a prayer on purpose. Just test it for six months and see how you do with it. If you're not happy with the results then give it up. I think it will make a believer out of you. There's a magic in believing. Good things happen when you believe. When you believe in God he will come into your life.

The American Indians used a form of prayer by dancing. They had a rain dance and a war dance and others. This was a form of prayer. They would sing or chant and dance in hopes of bringing rain and other goals. You don't have to dance to have your prayers answered. There are different types of prayer. You can recite prayers from a prayer book or make up your own as you go along. I believe that both ways are good but I prefer to make up my own. Repeating the same prayer over and over gets boring to me.

Another thing you can do is to help yourself accomplish your prayers. It's been said that the Lord helps those who help themselves. You have to do what you can to make the prayer come true. I used to hang out at a neighborhood bar when I was unemployed. All of the guys who came in knew each other and they knew that I wasn't working. They'd ask me if I had found a job and I'd say no; I've been in here all day drinking beer and no one has come over to offer me a job. It wasn't likely that anybody would. When I made up my mind to find work, I began looking and putting in applications. I found a job but I had to help myself to do it. Whenever I wanted a job I was able to find one even in a small town I had two jobs, but that was about the limit of available employment in the small town that I was in. If it's a job you're looking for you're going to find them scarce in small towns. Somebody has the job and there's a list of their relatives waiting to get the job when they quit. You will do a lot better in finding a job in a big city. In the small town you will compete against someone who everybody has known personally for years. A man in a small Missouri town was more than well-qualified for a job as a cafeteria chef in the local school. He had over twenty years experience as a chef in institutional cooking. His opposition could cook but had far less experience. He knew everybody in the town and he got the job over someone with much more impressive qualifications. For a small town it's the old story of who do you know.

Are all of our actions of a selfish nature? Even prayer? I once had a big argument. I said that if you helped a dog that was stuck in a fence it wouldn't be selfish. The reply was if you didn't help the dog you would have felt guilty so helping the dog was selfish. The argumentative lady had the idea that even if you did it for someone or something else it satisfied a need of yours; so therefore it was selfish. I don't agree, but you must admit it's a good argument. If you ask someone else to pray for you it's selfish. Even if all of our actions are selfish we needn't be ashamed. Your No. 1 rule in life should be to look out for No. 1 and then your family. If you don't take care of yourself and stand up for your rights, who will?

I remember the big prayers in my life. One of the earliest prayers that I remember occurred when the school had a picnic at an amusement park in St. Louis. I was about seven years old and since my mother worked, she made arrangements with my cousin to take care of me. When we first got there I got some money from my cousin that Mother had given her. It wasn't long before I used it all up at the shooting gallery. Well, I couldn't get any more money until my mother got there later in the day. I decided to go swimming and it was O.K. with my cousin. She warned me to stay out of the deep water. I changed and was looking the pool over. I went back and forth trying to decide which was the shallow end of the pool. Well, I found it O.K. and jumped in. I found myself in the deep end going up and down. I'd sink to the bottom and give a push and come to the top. When my head came up above the water I could hear the music in the park and then it would go away as I went to the bottom again. I was raised Catholic and prayed to St. Michael who was my personal saint. I went up and down for what seemed to be a long time and finally a nice young man jumped in and pulled me. He pointed out the shallow end and told me that I'd be better off to stay there. He didn't have to tell me twice. I thanked him and headed for the shallow end. The rest of the swimming session was a good one. Later that day my mother showed up from work and we had a good time. I got to shoot the gun again after she got there and was happy.

Another time, a man asked me to get in his car with him and I did. He was up to no good and I said a prayer and told him that I wanted out. My door handle didn't work so I was trapped. He let me out and I went on my way. I was lucky that my prayer was answered. I could have wound up kidnapped or dead.

My biggest answered prayer was for a son who had the same birthday as mine. We were in the hospital the day before my birthday and I could feel the presence of the Lord. I was constantly asking him to let it happen. Give me a son who had the same birthday as mine. The next day came and sure enough I got a son on my birthday. I named him Michael after one of my church names and after St. Michael who had been good to me on several occasions. I felt it was the least that I could do after this minor miracle. I'm praying now that my wife and I get to move into a larger house so that we can regain custody of her children. I know that God won't let me down. I just have to wait for things to happen in our lives. There are others praying for this goal so I know that it will happen in time.   We're just now listing the place we live in for sale and we've started looking towards the time to sell. We've picked out several new places to live in. More later!

Chapter 4

POSTIVE THINKING

You may or may not have given much thought to the type of thinking that you do most. There are two kinds: Positive and Negative. Positive is far superior to negative. They both influence your life. They are equal in power. If you indulge in negative thinking, negative things will occur in your life. On the other hand if you indulge in positive thinking positive things will happen in your life. I won't go as far as some writers and say that this is foolproof. You can have a positive attitude about becoming a millionaire and unless you act on the proper idea to attain this goal, all you'll have is a positive attitude. You could have accumulated some amount of wealth but not have reached your goal of one million. Even part of the goal wouldn't have been possible with the wrong attitude. Positive thinking is like the magic of believing. Without one of these factors you can have little chance for success. They go hand in hand. First you must believe that you can succeed and then with a positive mental attitude you must then take action to attain your goal. You will find it helpful to build a success consciousness in yourself. When you've had a few successes it will be easier to attain the next one. You can become very negative about positive thinking if you go about it the wrong way. if you're the average working guy and your first goal is to make a million in one year and you don't, you'll begin to doubt the principle. It's not the fault of the principle that you failed, it's your fault for setting a foolish goal. At least in the example we set a time period even if it was a short one. Many people wish they were millionaires but think about it in a vague way. They may say to a friend that they would rather be rich or some other vague thing. These wishes have a slim chance of coming true. Another goal may be to drive a new Cadillac or Mercedes or even a Rolls Royce. The average working person will likely never know these luxuries. I hope that I remember to stress this one point in every chapter. You're not going to get rich by working for the other guy on a typical job. Some jobs will pay well enough so that you do O.K. like a heavy equipment operator or a construction worker. Computers are good also. There are many good types of work that allow you to get ahead enough to have some money to invest in other things to build your fortune. Let's just say that you are making twenty-dollars an hour in 1985. With cost of living raises you will be getting more money in the future, but with inflation, everything will cost more so you'll probably be at the same rate even when the pay is forty dollars an hour. Your money will only buy as much then as $20.00 per hour will buy now. Twenty dollars per hour for a forty hour week is $800.00 per week or a bit more than $3,200.00 per month. If 30 percent is withheld for taxes, etc., your approximate monthly pay to spend would be $2,240.00.

Let's say that you could get by on $1,240.00 per month. That would leave you $1,000.00 per month to save or $12,000.00 per year. If you just put the money in a fruit jar and work for thirty years at the same rate you would have $360,000.00 after thirty years. The amount would be more because of raises, but the spending power would be about the same because of inflation. That's only about ⅓ of a million and you needed to be paid $20.00 per hour to do it. What chance do you think you'd have to accumulate that much money at $5.00 an hour? If you invested the money at a ten percent rate of interest, the total amount would triple in thirty years. If inflation grows at ten percent, the spending power will be the same then as it is today. If one of your goals is to be wealthy, you are going to need an angle that will work for you. I think that I've shown you that wages alone aren't enough. One big problem that we face is "the wolf at the door." The rent or house payment is due every month and there are other bills to pay as well — not to mention food, entertainment and the car. Most people are trained to think in terms of getting a job. Your parents tell you to go to school and get a good education so that you can get a good job. We're brainwashed into thinking that all you need in life is a good job. This is O.K. if you become a doctor or lawyer. There are few jobs that pay the kind of money we would like to have from a job.

You will have to set small goals and accomplish them to build success consciousness. If you don't want to get burned out on the idea that positive thinking really works, you will have to start small. If you earn aproximately $5.00 an hour, you could set a goal to save about $2,500.00 in one year. This is realistic. If you are in one of these low-paying jobs and you want to make more money, you may have to have training for a new job. This will likely require a sacrifice on your part. You can't go to school all day and work a job at the same time until your training is finished. When you are trained for the new job, life will get easier. You can cut back to 8 hours a day and now you'll be getting more money.

I believe in using capital to make capital. If you have money you can make money. Buying real estate can be very profitable. In as little as one month or less you could make $5,000.00 by buying a house or apartment and reselling it at a profit. The key to success here is to buy below market value so there is a profit margin immediately. It sounds easy and it is if you go about it in the right way. You need more money than just the down payment. You're responsible for the mortgage payments until you sell the property. You'll need to use some common sense in your dealings. For instance, if the condo market is depressed you wouldn't want to buy one and be stuck with it.

Many of the good self-help books talk about positive thinking. One book is entirely about positive thinking. It's that important. Many of the books that I've read left me curious — Maybe better informed but still curious. They cover one topic and one topic only. You have to read several books to get more information on the idea of making your life a better one. It's my intention to make this book more complete.

There are three ways to look at a thing. One view is optimistic or positive; another is pessimistic or negative; and the third is realistic which isn't either positive or negative. An optimistic looks at a half of a glass of water and says the glass is half full. The pessimist looks at the same glass of water and says it's half empty. The realist looks at it and says it's a half of a glass of water. It's all in the eye of the beholder. How do you see a half of a glass of water? You should see it as half full from today onward. Learn to be optimistic or positive in your thinking.

When I worked at Kirby Vacuum Cleaners in St. Louis County, we used to have meetings and during the meeting we would all sing. The boss would say that if you can't sing well sing loud. Everybody sang and it sounded pretty well. We had song books to guide us along. If you've never done this you can't know how good it makes you feel. It motivated us to be happy and it's easier to be positive when you're happy than when you're sad. If you're unhappy, a lot of the time you may want to work on the causes of why you're unhappy so that it will be easier to be positive. This would be a good idea. Work on the troubles in your life so that you can start being positive. Overhauling a car takes time and overhauling your life and habits will take time as well. You will have to be patient while you're building the new you. Remember that "Rome wasn't built in a day". If you get discouraged, you can pick this book up again and again to reinspire yourself. You don't really learn a thing until you've reviewed it five times or more. The first time you overhaul the car you should have an auto manual nearby to check as you go along. After a few times you won't need it anymore but it's nice to know that you have it just in case you need it. It's the same thing when you overhaul your life. You will need guidance. If you're not satisfied with your life. You will need guidance. If you're not satisfied with your life after you've followed the guidelines in this book you could get other books. Don't stop trying to have a better life. It's a worthwhile goal for anyone at any age from about 13 years old and up. Sometimes you have a thing explained to you several times or in a different way before you understand it. If this book does it all for you, then you won't need another one; but if not, read other books until you're satisfied with the outcome of your life.

I've always known some way to make money even when I was very young. A friend and I went around shining shoes when we were about ten years old. We went into a neighborhood bar and asked if anyone wanted their shoes shined. My friend took over and told the customer that I couldn't shine shoes as well as he could. I knew if I had the chance I could do as well as he or better. While I was thinking about the dirty trick my friend played on me, a man said, "I'll give you a chance." You can shine my shoes. I did a good job and he gave me a tip for my trouble. He was happy with the job that I had done. You see, I knew that I could do O.K. if I only had the chance and it came my way. We both made some extra money and by believing in myself I was rewarded. It was the positive attitude that helped me. You probably can think of a situation in your own life in which a positive attitude has helped you too. It works like magic. Remember to set easy goals to get a success consciousness so that the harder ones will be easier when you get to them. It's very important to go slow in the beginning. When I first learned about positive thinking I got all charged up and began thinking in terms of millions in a few weeks. I got burned out when I didn't get rich over night. I was too impatient. I set my goals too high in the beginning. The information that I got was general as you will find with most self-help books, tapes, or records. It took me years to develop my understanding of how things like prayer and positive thinking can work in your life. It cost me a lot of money to learn what I've learned. I spent about $250 on Earl Nightingale tapes about ten years ago or maybe it was closer to fifteen years ago. I got the idea from an associate who also was selling educational material in California. We were talking one day and he was telling me how his very successful father spent a lot of money on books and magazines and other educational materials. It struck me as a good thing to do. It was like a new door was opened me. The idea took on spectacular proportions and it's a simple principle that we all learn in school. Get a good education. At the time I associated a good education with formal schooling and the idea of doing it on your own was a novel one. You may be out of school but that doesn't stop you from learning. It's a good idea to continue your education after you're out of school. They don't teach self-help courses in school today; maybe someday they will realize the importance of this material and add it to the roster of subjects that are offered. It could even be made manditory. This could bring about a change in our thinking. The old way of getting a good education so that you can get a good job would be outdated. A new way of thinking would come true. Get a good education so it can help you get rich. We may never know the outcome of one of my conversations with a former associate. I held the view if everybody was rich; no one would work. No one would have to work and the country would go to pot. My learned friend disagreed with me. He said that many people would work to have something to do. I said they would all want the good jobs. He said no, since everyone was different. When you think about it I guess there would be someone to clean stables who likes being around horses and knew that the job had to be done. Cleaning stables is not a glamour job and I couldn't think why anyone with riches would want to do it. Being employed is a worthwhile activity regardless of the pay. If everyone were rich, everyone would not have the same tastes in jobs as well as other things. It stands to reason that people would want to work even if they were wealthy. They may want to work less hours than forty per week and that could work out O.K. too. I read that the most unhappy people were those who belonged to the jet set. After a while it got boring for them. They weren't doing anything worthwhile and so they got bored. Play is a good thing when it offsets work and vice versa. It's likely that you will have to be older to find this out from personal experience. You may someday get an inheritance. You could take a small percentage of the money and travel around the world. It would be fun for a while, but if you kept it up for a long time it would get boring to you. If you wanted to try this and keep the expenses down you could take short trips in the U.S.A. or whatever country you live in. Look at the stars who are on the road constantly. You may think it's a life of glamour, but if you get their view of life on the road, you'll find that it's not so rosy. They do make a lot of money but you wonder if it's all worth it. The kids are in school and can't travel with them, so they are a bit alone in their travels. What about a doctor? They make a lot of money but they pay the price for the privilege. Keep in mind what the price is for your new way of life. There are many ways to go about getting wealthy that aren't so taxing on your life. Writing is one way to make some money and it's easy. You can do it at home in your spare time. If you're good, you may be published the first time you do a book or article. You may be able to get into lyrics for songs, but that is tougher unless you can write the music as well. There are a lot of rip-offs in the song-writing business. If you do get a song, don't pay anyone to publish it. The publisher should pay you. There's a book called the *Songwriters Market* and it lists publishers and gives information about them and what they are looking for. There's another book called the *Writer's Market* and it lists book publishers and what they are interested in. It's not as hard as you think if you're good. There are many ways to get something extra going in your life. These are only a few. Whatever you do you will do it better with a positive attitude. Use a positive attitude in all aspects of your life and see how much better it is.

Chapter 5

BELIEVING

There's magic in believing. No matter what it is you can make it true by believing it. If you believe in God you give this belief credit just by believing it. When you believe a thing is possible by believing that it is then it is. Stay away from words like impossible. Instead use words like improbable. You may get an argument such as you can't bar-b-que ice. That's a good argument but you can bar-b-que ice it just melts and there's nothing left. You could say that you can't eat bar-b-qued ice, but if you put a bowl in the pit you could catch the melted ice and consume it. Eating it or drinking it is a matter of semantics or a play on words. You could put it in your mouth and make a chewing motion and say that you ate it. Then you look at a thing as improbable you leave room for the idea that it still is possible. It's like the optimist and the pessimist. It's all in your way of thinking. The first step to success is to believe a thing is possible. If you believe that it's possible then it is. If you believe it's impossible then that's true also. It works both ways. You will be amazed at the things you can accomplish when you believe in yourself and your ability. I never vaulted as high as my companion in high school because he believed he could go eight feet and not knock down the bar and I had my doubts. I don't think that I ever made the eight foot mark when I pole vaulted in high school. Since my companion could go higher than me, he got to compete in track meets with other schools and I did not. That's just one example of believing. I should say two examples. My companion believed that he could do it and I believed that I couldn't. I wasn't outstanding in high school in any of the sports, as my confidence then was less than it is now. I had trouble believing in myself. I had an inferiority complex. This hurt me in more ways than one. Intramural wrestling was my best sport and I never competed with any other schools in that. I did get a patch for my high school sweater and was proud of it. When a girl that I liked wore it, it made me proud. It was one of my few successes. I failed 11th grade and felt badly about repeating the year over, so I decided to join the Army. A buddy and I signed up together in October 1959. We encountered peace time service through our entire tour of duty. Out of the four of us who looked into paratrooper training, I was the only one to go into the paratroopers. The friend that went in with me didn't pass the physical and of the other two guys, only one passed and he didn't go in, so the other guy wouldn't feel bad. Your confidence is built in the Army. They even have a course called the confidence course. This is in basic training. Everyone goes through basic training when they join the Army. From basic training you can go a number of places. I went to advanced infantry training at Ft. Benning Georgia. When we signed up the recruiting Sergeant told us to tell the commanding officer that we wanted to go into the 101st airborne and he would take care of it for us. I got my first clue that we weren't going to do much talking when we were sworn in. Everything was peaches and cream until then. Right after the man said that we were officially in the Army he got gruff and said now sit down shut up and no smoking. Well, while I was at Ft. Benning I found out that we all would get orders from nigher up as to where we were going when we finished advanced infantry training. The day finally came and when I read the orders by my name, I was disappointed. I was being sent to Ft. Bragg, North Carolina to the 82nd airborne. There was no comparison in the insignia of the two units. The 101st had a bald-headed eagle on their patch and the 82nd only had a couple of A's. We went right to the company where we would be permanently stationed and while the rest of the company was busy with their duties as airborne soldiers we went to school. The first week of jump school was half a day of exercise. It was four weeks all together and we ran everywhere we went. We ran forever. My side used to hurt and I longed to fall out by the side of the road and rest, but I kept on going. In time it got so that when we quit running I was ready to go on longer. I guess the smoke cleared out of my lungs and I could run better. We got punishment for the dumbest reasons and they laid it on heavy. You'd do ten push-ups and they'd use trick questions to trip you up like, "How many weeks in a day?" You answer quickly, "seven." When they repeated your answer, you realized that you made a mistake and they would say get down and do ten more. Many of those exercise sessions would be very tiring and they'd ask you if you wanted to quit. "Do you want to sign a quit slip?" they'd say. It was about the toughest thing that I'd ever done in my life, but I did it. My C.O. in basic wore airborne wings and when I asked him if he thought that I could do it he said "I did it, so can you". I started believing from that moment on and stuck with it. We had completed our training and the graduation ceremony was going on. When the Colonel came up to me and put my wings on my chest I felt ten feet tall. I had had my doubts along the way, but deep down there was that belief that I could do it and I did it. This one major success was the turning point in my life. I had learned to go the extra mile. Do all that you can, then do one more for airborne. When we did ten pushups we really did eleven. One was for airborne. It was a custom. It taught me the principle of going the extra mile. It pays off in the long run. Airborne training is positive. Someone you might know in the public eye who was in an airborne unit when he was in service is Coach Don Coreyelle of the San Diego Chargers football team. He was formerly with St. Louis and they haven't been the same since he left. It was my belief that kept me going in a tough training program when I was in the army. It was worth it, but I would have never made it without the belief that I could do it. If you're going to accomplish anything, you first have to believe that you can do it or you're beat before you get started. By the way after I was in the 82nd airborne for a while, I became quite proud of the insignia. It took on a special luster after all of the work and blood and sweat that went into the privilege of wearing it. I believe in prayer and many of my prayers have been answered. I told you about Michael who has the same birthday as me. That answered prayer bolsters my faith in God. Any answered prayer should bolster your faith. If you say enough prayers, you're bound to get some of them answered.

One reason that I live where I live is because of belief. They told me that I'd never get my price for my old house in St. Louis but I did. I had had real estate training and knew the ways to evaluate the value of a house. I had 3 choices for a new location: Vegas or L.A. or Florida. My wife picked Florida. We made a home-hunting trip and found a nice home in Homestead, Fl. I'm remarried now to a much nicer lady. Sometimes I wish we could have met years ago, but this may be how destiny works in one's life. If we'd met years ago, the things that have occured wouldn't have occured. My last two children would not have been born and her three children wouldn't have been born. We wouldn't trade any of them in on new ones so things had to unfold the way they did for them to turn out like they are. There are unseen forces working in your life and they usually know what is best for you. Sometimes no matter how hard you try to get a thing done, it won't get done. We can only try to do it the way we think it should be done and live with the outcome. Sometimes what you think is best isn't best at all and the Lord is looking out for you. Sometimes he lets you do it your way. Maybe he does it to teach us a lesson. Remember I told you that there are mysteries in life. You may not understand all of the mysteries, but you can be aware that they exist. The main thing is to learn the principles that can help you and put them to work in your life. You can build a success consciousness about believing by listing the things you believe and have believed over the years. Go back as far as you can remember and work your way to the present time. You may be surprised at all of the things that you've believed in over the years. List the little things as well as the big ones. When you had a dog and you called his name you believed that he would come to you. When you went out to start the car you believed that it would start right up and you'd be on your way with no problem. Most of the time this was true, at least for me it was.

Chapter 6

CAUSE AND EFFECT

Cause and effect is just one more thing that you should be aware of in your life. For every effect there is a cause. You may have learned a little about this in a physics class in school. The rotation of the earth causes the ocean tides to ebb and flow. You may understand the terminology that for every action there is an opposite and equal reaction. This works in life as well as in physics. If you're not an evil person you may not have too much negativeness in your life, but you may know someone who does a lot of bad things and see the effects in their life. You remember that we said you get out of life what you put into it in a previous chapter. Well, this is another way of saying that very thing only it may be a little easier to understand. It's easy enough to understand the principles of physics when they are explained to you and the principles of cause and effect work in the same way. We can use a previous example to further explain the principle. You remember the guy who cheated on his wife and found out that his girl friend was pregnant by someone else? He was heartbroken. How did all of this come to be? Well, first there was the cause and then there was the effect. He did his wife wrong by cheating on her. That was the cause. The unhappy news that he received from his girlfriend was the effect. Cause and effect differ from action and reaction because of the time periods involved. In physics an action is followed right away by a reaction. With cause and effect the reaction can be delayed for a long time. The two principles are alike, but the time period is different in most cases. We're going to use another example ιo help you understand the principle better. In the case of the guy who stole an electrical extension cord there also was a delay in the time it took for the reaction. It was about two weeks before he got the ticket for a traffic violation. You never know how long it will take for the re-action. He could have been caught red handed on the job and fired on the spot. Had that happened it might have been clearer to him that you get paid for whatever you do in life. I don't think that he's aware of any of these principles to this day. If he's still doing these type of deeds today thinking he's going to get ahead by cheating and stealing he'll never have a trouble free life. When your high school teachers told you not to cheat on a test, you may have thought that they were wrong. They may have said don't cheat because you'll only be cheating yourself. Well, how could making a better score hurt you? When the Test came and you didn't know the answer, you cheated yourself by copying it from someone else. You should have studied so that you would know the answer when the time came. I don't believe in cheating of any kind, but you must admit that if you learned the answer for all time when you saw it on someone else's paper, you got a little bit smarter by learning the answer. I don't recommend this method of learning to anyone. When I was in high school I goofed off and made poor grades because of it. I had the intelligence but didn't use it properly. I still got somewhat of an education just by being there. The teachers would go over the material in class and you could learn by hearing the information. I must have learned something because just before I got out of the Army I had a chance to take the G.E.D. high school equivalency test and did so well that they wanted me to take the college test. I got too busy to take the college test, but later took the entrance exam for a junior college in California and did so well in English that they put me in an advanced English course right away. The cause for this would be paying attention in class and a good IQ. Speaking of I.Q., there are those experts who think that your I.Q. doesn't change. I disagree with them. Here's why: When I took the test for the Army I made a score of 119. To go into officers training you needed a score of 125 or better. I didn't make it by 6 points, but after the test was over they went over a few of the trick questions and told us the answers. I had trouble with one and got it wrong. The question was "How far can you go into a woods"? Well I was on the right track, but couldn't put the answer in the right way. I reasoned that if the woods was one mile you could go in for a half of a mile. They got me confused by not saying how big the woods were well it turned out that it doesn't matter if you have the right answer. The correct answer is half way in. The other half would be out no matter how big the woods were. Now since they give you so many points for each right answer to compute your I.Q., I was now smarter and would have made a higher grade if I took the test over because I knew more correct answers. Even this one answer I just went over would have raised my grade so my I.Q. was higher. Well that's my argument for those who think you can't raise your I.Q.

Getting back to cause and effect — The automobile accident. There are accidents and there are close calls that just miss. You can trace the cause to the person who is at fault if you get a good look at the occurence. Sometimes the person at fault is long gone for the near miss or accident. I hang out at a restaurant that has a glass front and you can get a good view of the street. I see near misses all of the time. Once in a while there is an accident. The latest one that I remember was right outside of the place. A man who was involved came in to call the police and he said it was the other driver's fault. It wasn't, but no one argued with him. He soon found out that it was his fault after the police got there. I guess underwriters are all too familiar with cause and effect. You could hit another car and not be at fault. I hit a car a few years ago and the other driver was at fault. The driver turned in front of me because his vision was partially impaired by the car along side me. He thought the way was clear. When I saw him I hit the brakes but rammed him in the side. The policeman was nice enough not to give the man a ticket for causing the accident even though he was at fault. He hadn't yielded the right of way to me and by pulling in front of me so close, he cut my brake reaction time too short and the effect caused the accident. There are all kinds of examples of cause and effect and action and reaction. Look for some examples in your everyday life. It's nice to be informed. The more you know, the better you will be.

Chapter 7

BLACK MAGIC

The term black magic has a mystical quality to it. It conjures up images of witches standing over a brewing pot with steam erupting from it. Some of the witches throughout history may have practiced magic and had good luck with the results. I believe in black magic as well as white magic I had an experience with black or white magic in my last marriage. I was very upset with the prospect of dissolving that marriage and there seemed to be no reasoning with my wife at the time. I didn't know what to do to save the marriage, so I called a friend who I found out knew about black magic and white magic. She told me that someone had put a curse on me and I'd have to take steps to nullify it. She told me to get a magnet and put it in a wine glass and fill the glass with water. I was to place it in the closet in our bedroom. This would help stop my wife from being so negative. It seemed to work a little. My wife seemed calmer, but she still insisted on a divorce. We ended up getting a divorce. I still think that the magnet in the glass of water helped but I supposed that I would have needed something stronger. I'm over the heartache now and happily remarried to a nice lady. I didn't know enough about black or white magic to get the job done, but I'm sure that it could have been done with the right formula. One other thing my friend told me to look out for was someone who might have placed a broom outside the door. This would help the person who cast a spell on me to get me out of the house. Apparently there are a number of mechanical things involved in black magic Since I'm not an expert on the subject I can only advise you of my beliefs that black and white magic do work. These are just two more examples of the unforeseen forces that go on in every day life. Most books written on the subject are done on black magic and not white magic. If you do find out about these things I strongly suggest that you use white magic in your life. Black magic uses the forces of evil to do it's work and white magic uses the forces of good to do it's work. You may be able to interchange the spells listed in a black magic book so that you're actually practicing white magic instead of black. They both work in the same way. Don't be afraid to buy a book on black magic so that you can learn about it. You can do the same thing with white magic as you can with black. It may be tempting to put a curse on a friend or enemy but just remember that another law of life will come into play after you've put a curse on someone. You get out of life what you put into it and it could just turn out that the evil deed that you wished for your friend or enemy will backfire and come true in your own life. If this doesn't happen, something else will come into your life that you won't be too pleased with. Use only white magic if you use any all.

Chapter 8

HOROSCOPE

I think that everybody is familiar with astrology in one way or another. You can find your daily horoscope in the newspaper or you can get a book that deals with only people of your sign. Most of the horoscope predictions that we come in contact with are general and of little use. They're good for amusement. Sometimes they say you will have a financial gain and it's payday and you think that the writer is all-knowing. Your horoscope may say that you are going to take a short trip. Well you probably go to work and that could be the short trip. Most of these predictions are general in nature as they have to fit a lot of people. They're amusing at best. If you want to get a true idea of what lies ahead for you, you should have a personal chart done with the astrologer using all of the proper information. You'll need to know your time of birth and the place of your birth as well as the date. With this information you can get a personal chart done for a fee. If you can get it done for free, you're lucky. I could have had my chart done when I lived in L.A. I met a man who had made a living as a professional astrologer and I learned something from him that I'll share with you. He told me that he had given up the profession because of the power he had over the people who came to him. He was a wise man and knew of the power of your thoughts. When he wrote out a personal horoscope for someone they took it and read it as if it were gospel and because they believed it came true for them. They must have thought that my friend was a wizard. The fact is they could have written the horoscope themselves the way they wanted their life to turn out and it would have turned out that way. It's the same thing for palmists and tarot readers. You can forecast your life the same as they can only you can do it better. If one of the predictions for your future is that you will have three kids you can make this come true in your life if you believe it. If you're a woman and have had those three children you could cause your body to get a headache on your fertile nights and avoid conception in this way. Ever want to skip school and find yourself getting sick so that you could stay home when you felt fine just a few moments before? It just goes to show you how strong the power of believing is. Don't let someone else write your future for you; do it yourself. Be your own astrologer or palmist or tarot reader. I'm not saying that the horoscope has no use. I think that it does. One of the things that you can find in a book on horoscope for your sign is who is compatible with you and who is not. It is my belief that if you and your mate are compatible through your horoscope, you will stay together longer than if you pick a mate of non-compatible sign.

I wish that I could get statistics on this, but so far I haven't been able to get any information. If you are curious too you could get a book on horoscope that lists who is compatible with who and check it out with friends and relatives. I know I was glad to know that my wife has a compatible sign with mine. So far as I can tell from my own experience, it's working. My three other marriages were with signs that were not compatible with mine. All three of them failed. This one is kind of new but we get along better than I've ever gotten along with any of the others. Before you take a mate or another mate I think that you owe it to yourself to check this idea out and see if it seems to work. If you find that it works for others you would want to pick your next mate from your three compatible signs. I'm a Scorpio and my wife is a Cancer. As I said we are compatible according to the book I bought on horoscopes. Some people don't believe anything about horoscopes is true, but I think it has some merit. Hitler was a fanatic about horoscopes. He had a personal astrologer on his staff. Hitler didn't check with his astrologer one day and something bad happened that might have been avoided if he had been forewarned about it.

If you are a doubter, I'd advise you to check it out and see if you can find anything good about it. Do this with an open mind. This is not only a good idea for horoscopes, but with anything. I used to hear something bad about someone I knew in high school but I reserved my final judgement until I had checked it out and many times I found that what had been said wasn't true at all. I'd keep this bit of gossip in my mind and I was a stickler for remembering exactly what was said. This is a good quality for you to have. It seems that a lot of people get it all mixed up. They told a joke on a TV program to a bunch of different people and asked them to repeat it and when it was told by them they made one mistake or another. The joke was about a doctor who cut off all four of a frog's legs one at a time and said to the frog, jump and he did until he cut the last foot off. He cut the last foot off. He cut off the foot not the leg. That's the same mistake almost everybody made when they retold the joke. They said leg instead of foot. Well, when the frog failed to jump the doctor wrote in his notes that if you cut off all of a frog's feet, he goes deaf. It just goes to show you that you have to pay close attention to get the facts correct.

You can look at horoscope in a new light now. When you see it in the newspaper you can read it for the amusement of it.

Chapter 9

PHILOSOPHY

Some philosophical discussions can be a bit silly. A friend of mine took a course in philosophy. He explained how we don't really exist and proved it verbally. Well, regardless of his proof we know that we do exist. We are flesh and bones and a whole lot more. This is only one aspect of philosophy. Having a philosophy on life is another. This is my main concern: your philosophy of life. Your outlook on life is important. It colors your whole life. A person with a good philosophy will have a good life and a person with a poor philosophy will have a poor life. It's like anything else. You make the choice of whether you have a good outlook or a poor one. If you never knew this before you know it now and can do something to make your life a better one. Your outlook on life is just another habit. Habits can be changed. You can replace a bad habit with a good one. First you should make a list of all of your habits. Then separate the good ones from the bad ones. When you're finished you should have two lists — One with your good habits on it and one with your bad habits on it. These habits should relate to your outlook on life. Some of the other lists that you make from time to time will have other habits on them, but this list should concentrate on philosophy. Once you've finished the lists you should look them over and decide which of your habits you are going to keep and which ones you are going to replace and which ones you are simply going to eliminate from your life. When you finish with these changes you should have a new self image and a healthy one at that. Your self image is important and it should be a good one. A typical philosophy on life should include a variety of things. A good relationship with God, a healthy regard for your fellow man and a positive attitude are only a few of the things that should be included. Let the golden rule be a guïde in your life. For those of you who aren't familiar with the Golden Rule it goes like this: " Do unto others as you would have others do unto you." This will help keep negative things out of your life. That's because you get out of life what you put into it. This was discussed in a former chapter and you should be well-aware of it by now. The Golden Rule is the only sensible way to avoid useless pain and suffering in your life. If you do no evil deeds to your fellow man then no evil deeds will happen in your life. At least on the basis of as ye sew so shall ye reap. There are unseen forces in everybody's life and some small evil may creep in. This will be minimal if you lead a good life and have a good philosophy on life. For some things there's no rhyme or reason. I don't understand the cruelity of a person who has no arms or legs or is paralized and confined to a wheelchair, but I know there is a reason. I can't think of a good reason for this hardship to be in anybody's life, but it does exist. It may be that some good comes from these afflictions. Consider the case of someone who is blind. You may have heard the same thing that I did about people who are blind. They develop a sixth sense. The example that I'm familiar with is a blind person sitting in on a church service. They could be blind and deaf also. You would think that they would get no benefit from the service but because of their sixth sense they can feel the vibrations going on and get an understanding of what is happening. The experience isn't a total waste for one of these people. Sometimes if they have a positive attitude, they can have an advantage over the ordinary person. How could that be you might ask? Well let me explain their advantage. You see, because of their handicap they have to try harder to succeed in life and the momentum that they attain by trying harder carries over into other things in their life. It's harder to move 50 pounds than it is to move 25 pounds; so if you have to move 25 pounds and someone else has to move 50 pounds, they have to try harder. This extra effort sets a tempo in their life. The normal person is moving the 25 pound load and the handicapped person has to move the 50 pound load. It's all in what you get used to. It takes more effort to move the 50 pound load, but it's all in what you get used to that matters. It's the same principle that I said they teach you in the army airborne. Go the extra mile; lift the heavier load. Try a little harder and it will pay off for you in the long run.

There's an old saying that goes "Don't put all of your eggs in one basket." This advocates diversification and it's a good idea. Well people are amazed with great statements and there's another one that goes, "Put all of your eggs in one basket; then watch the basket." Well these are two points of view and they are opposite. They both work but I prefer diversification. I don't put all of my eggs in one basket. If you put all of your eggs in one basket so to speak, you may have made a bad investment and you're stuck with it. If it turns out to be an excellent investment, you're lucky and as well off as can be. With diversification you have more chances for one or more of your investments to turn out good. You've got more going for you with diversification. I'll get more into investments in a later chapter. This is another aspect in your outlook on life — a part of your philosophy. This is an important part of your financial picture. Give this aspect of your life your most careful attention.

A complete philosophy will give you a good healthy outlook on life and your life will be a better one because of it. Prejudice is something that you should eliminate from your life. It means to pre-judge. It's not fair to you to do this. You should get all of the facts before you make any judgement about anything. Use a scientific approach when making decisions.

Chapter 10

MORALS

Ethics and morals are the same thing. Ethics is one definition of morals. Morals deals with right conduct. That is to say right behavior. It even applies to sexual behavior. A person with loose morals is said to be liberal with sex. Poor morals applies to your everyday conduct. It can also apply to business dealings. All of your moral practices should be on the up and up, above board and ethical. If you are involved in business practices, you should strive to be fair to all parties concerned. This is one of the four rules I learned in high school from a bulletin board. It has stuck with me all of these years. Is it fair to all concerned? If it isn't, it isn't ethical. The term ethical fits in better with business than morals. I'm sure that you've heard someone speak of one business deal or another and use the term ethical rather than moral. Morals apply well to conduct and sexual behavior. Until I looked up the term moral in the dictionary, I though that it was only applied to sex. In my younger years I used the term morals in connection with sexual behavior exclusively. This is O.K. It is one of the definitions of the term.

All of your moral habits should be good in nature. It's like the other chapters where you made a list or two. To bring your life nearer to perfection you will want to have only good moral habits. Start by making a list of your good habits and a list of your bad ones. Arrange the list of your bad habits with the easiest one to change on the top. You remember that it is easier to succeed when your first goal is an easy one. The more goals you attain, the easier it gets for you. It makes it easier to accomplish the harder ones when you're success conscious. You can make it easier by making your lists in three categories: No. 1 is personal relationships; No. 2 is sex habits; No. 3 is business practices. These are the main areas where morals are concerned. List the bad habits with the easiest one to change at the top of the list and begin working at the top of the list. You may not want to bother with making a list, but I assure you it's the best way. You may be able to do it without making a list but it's best to list an idea when it's fresh in your mind. I'll show you what I mean. Did you ever have your mind on something and then in a few minutes forget what it was completely. You try to remember, but you can't. If you put the idea in your mind and say to yourself that you want to remember what it was that you forgot it will come back to you in time. But that's the point. Why be at the mercy of your mind to bring back the idea when it's good and ready? If you write it down, you merely have to look at it to remember.

Ideas are like a sly old deer. First you see him in plain view and the next thing you know he's gone for good. You may see h:.n again, but you may not. It's like that with ideas. You have to write them down on a piece of paper so that they don't get away like the deer. It's a bit of a pain to write all of your ideas down just when they come to you but if you don't they can get away from you. I heard of a man who had a pen and paper near his bedside so that if he got an idea in the middle of the night he could write it down and capture it forever. I've had a general idea of what I want to put into this book, but I've had to wait for the deer to appear again and I had to stop writing and try and remember what came next. After a while I got smart and wrote it down. The last three chapters were writter down so that I could remember them easily. All that I had to do is look on the piece of paper where I wrote them. I've just listed six chapters to do after this one. It will be easy to know what to do next. When I've finished them   I'll have to think up the next ones and write them down. I know that I'm going to do chapters on finance and related subjects when I get further along with the book. I feel that most self-help books are too general. This should be the most complete self-help book on the market when I get finished with it.

Chapter 11

CHARACTER

Your character is like your personality. It's who you are. Part of your character can be inherited from either of your parents or both of them. A person of good character is a person of good repute. Or to say it another way this person is said to have a good reputation. When you talk about character you should know what makes up your character. As I said, it's similar to your personality and personality is made up from all of your habits. With character, some of your traits can be inherited from parents so that you have always had them. It's like instinct in animals. But just because you didn't acquire all of your habits doesn't mean that you can't change them. You may not want to change all of your habits. Some of them are good ones and shouldn't be changed. Even the worst person has some good traits. No one is totally rotten although you might know someone who runs a close second to rotten through and through. Again I'm going to suggest that you make two lists. You may wonder why I say that you should make two lists when you're only going to change the habits on the bad list of habits. Well there is a reason for this. It's a good reason too . If you just make one list, you only get a look at your bad traits and can get negative or down in the dumps. This isn't good for you. When you see the list with your good traits on it you feel a little better than if you only looked at the negative traits. At least you have some good points to lift your spirits. Don't take short cuts and make one list. Do it right and make two lists. By making the lists you will spend less time trying to remember your habits than if you try to do it from memory. Writing it down is a time saver.

Another definition of character is a role played by an actor or actress. The truth of the matter is that we're all actors and actresses in every day life. When you're dating a person you want to make a good impression so you may change your personality a bit to please them. If you're in a bad mood and have to face the public you may act as if you weren't in a bad mood so as not to offend the person with whom you are dealing. It could be a waitress in a restaurant or a shoe salesman. You want to be at your best and sometimes you have to act happy even though deep down you're not. At one time or another all of us have done some acting. When you tell a joke you act as the moderator. You hope people will laugh at the joke so that you feel that you have done a good job of telling it to them. Did you ever get a present that you didn't like and had to act like it was great so that you didn't hurt anybody's feelings? When you go on a job interview you put on your best behavior to impress the interviewer. If he said have you ever stolen anything you wouldn't tell him about the ash tray you got in Vegas. We're all actors. It's part of character.

Chapter 12

PERSONALITY

Your personality is an assemblage of your qualities, both good and bad. It's what makes you you. Everyone is different. You can say that there must be two people alike somewhere in the world and there may be. If you list all of the possible personality traits that a person can have, you will probably get at least eight or more. With just eight traits there are 336 possible combinations of these traits. That is to say that 336 people with only three traits each would all be different. I came by this information from my gambling habits. When you bet a trifecta with eight teams or eight horses or dogs competing, there are three hundred and thirty six combinations possible. You have to pick the first three to finish in that order. Each number that you add increases the total number of possible combinations. If you had nine traits, the total number of combinations would increase a lot. More so for ten and up. Since there are over 200 million people in this country alone it seems likely that there are duplicate personalities.

Personality is in relationship with your behavior. How you get along with others and your honesty, morals and personal habits are a few of your personality traits. People with a good personality get on well with others and people with a poor personality don't get along well with others. Do you have few friends in your life? Well this could be because of your personality. If you want more friends you will have to change your personality to a more pleasing one so that you can attract people into your life. Make two lists of your good and personality traits and put the easy to change ones on top of the bad traits list. Work on the first one and down the list until you've changed them all. Don't feel badly if you don't succeed in changing all of them. Nobody's perfect. I had an argument about whether a person could attain perfection in their life. The pro of it was that we are made in God's image and likeness and if God is perfect why couldn't a mortal be too? The con of it was that God never intended for us to be perfect. You can make up your own mind about which argument is right. One thing is for sure though: You can become a better person even if not perfect.

There are three aspects to personality. No. 1. How do you see yourself? No. 2. How do others see you? No. 3. How are you really? All three of these views can be the same or two can be the same or all of them can be different from one another. It would be a good idea to find out what these three views are. You can easily know how you see yourself and you can get the opinions of your friends and family as to how they see you. For how you really are you'll have to make a decision on that and try to make it an accurate one.

Chapter 13

DRUGS

We've all heard the term drugs at one time or another. There are three types of drugs: Prescription drugs, non-prescription drugs, and illegal drugs. Drugs of one kind or another have been around for centuries. Today there are many drugs available to us. If you happen to be one of those people who take illegal drugs you are messing up your life. There are all kinds of risks with illegal drugs. At least two major ones come to mind right away. One is that if you aren't careful you could take an overdose and end up dead. Two is you could get caught by the police with the illegal drugs and go to jail. It's the same with drugs as it is with anything. If you take too much it's no good for you. The Bible comments on this also. Roughly put it says "Eat not to excess and drink not to excess, in all things be moderate". Drinking too much will make you drunk. Eating too much will make you sick. It's best to regulate your consumption to moderate portions. This applies to drugs. If you continue to take illegal drugs, you should do it moderately only. It's my strong advice that you stop taking illegal drugs. From time to time we need the help of drugs in our lives. Even with the legal kind you have to exercise caution. Many people have died from taking too many drugs whether they were legal or illegal. Even non-prescription drugs can do a great deal of harm if not taken properly. Some people become addicted to the legal drugs and need to break this habit. Like all medicine, drugs should be taken only as prescribed or by label directions. The miracle of these pills can only work properly when you follow directions to the letter. Another common practice to save time or money or both is pill swapping. You get a prescription for a condition and a friend or relative gets the same or similar condition and you play doctor and offer them your prescription. This is bad. Their condition may be different from yours in some way and the pills do more harm than good. If this happens instead of giving them your pills have them see a doctor or maybe the pharmacist can give you a non-prescription medicine for them. It's better to seek advice of a professional than to play doctor yourself.

The bad habits you have concerning drugs will have to be eliminated if you are to improve your life. It's as easy as changing any other habit. All you have to do is make up two lists with the good habits on one and the bad habits on another one. List the habits that are easier to change at the top of your list of habits and start to work on changing them today. There are many chapters in which I suggest that you make two lists. If you try to do it all at once, you're going to have a lot of lists and maybe think that the job is too big, so do these lists and changes one chapter at a time.

Chapter 14

TWO SURVIVORS

This chapter is food for thought. It's to show you our dependency on other people. Have you ever said or heard someone say something like "I wish I were the only person on earth". What would it be like to be the only two people on the earth? Let's say that you have your choice of anyone you wish to be left here on earth with you. You can pick a movie star or rock singer. Anyone you like. Now the two of you are left here alone. How are you going to survive? How long do you think that you can survive? You can live anywhere you want to. Almost every house and apartment is furnished. If you're like me you'd pick the sun belt to avoid the harshness of winter. Transportation won't be a problem if the electric plants operate automatically. This would provide the power to pump the gas you will need to get around in the car of your choice. If it breaks down, all you have to do is go to a dealers lot and pick up another one. So transportation won't be a problem. Let's say that there is enough electricity to last you a lifetime stored up in the electric company's batteries. You could spend some of your time turning off lights in stores that you don't use. If a store you visit is dark, you can turn on the lights for the duration of your visit. You could cook with natural or bottled gas until it ran out. If that happened you could move to another place where the stove and heat is electric. You'd have power for the T.V. but no one to run the T.V. station. So you couldn't watch T.V. You could go to a store and pick up a video tape machine and get some pre-recorded movies and show them on T.V. You would have little use for money; although, any amount would be available to you. You could be a millionaire with lots of cash, but it would be useless to you. Everything would be free. In a matter of a month all of the dairy products at the store would have spoiled and of no use to you. A lot of the food would spoil in time. After six months you couldn't want to eat any of the meat in stores. You could survive for years on can goods. You could turn off all of the lights in stores except the ones you used. When you've used up all of the food from a store you could turn out all of the lights and start getting your supplies from another store where you turn on the lights. The same thing goes for the gas station where you get gas. When you use up all of the gas in the underground tanks you could close down that station and open up another one. The two of you may decide to repopulate the earth so you'd begin having children. You'd have to deliver the babies yourself as there would be no doctors available. By the time the first baby came you would need milk to feed him or her. You may get by with mother's milk but after a few children are born, you'd need fresh milk and the milk in the stores would have spoiled. You'll have to resort to basics and find a cow or two and a place nearby to put it. Then one of your daily chores would be to milk the cows to get fresh milk. Many animals in captivity would die because they would be penned up and there would be no one to feed them. This would be unavoidable. Even if you freed the caged animals it would take too long to get to all of them and many would die. Wild ones and horses and cattle that are on grazing lands could survive. You'd have to eat all of your meals at home or fix them yourself if you went to a restaurant as there would be no one to take your order. The days of ordering a Big Mac would be gone forever. No fancy dinners at a fancy restaurant. No movies. Little entertainment. You could find ways to amuse yourselves, but they would be limited. You would have to teach the children their school work as there would be no teachers to do it for you. We're taking for granted that the water system is on automatic also so you will have easy access to water. For fresh meat you will have to be a hunter and then a butcher once you've found fresh meat. Your life will be full of activities related to basic survival. The cuts of meat you get from a cow won't look like the ones you used to get at the store but they would be edible. If you've gotten a taste for turkey or duck or chicken, you'll have to kill the bird and pluck all of the feathers. Then you'll have to dress it and get it ready for cooking. Beef and pork will have to be skinned and cleaned and then butchered before you can cook it. If want to be involved in religion you'll have to be the preacher and refer to the Bible and prayer books. There will be no Sunday services to attend. No Broadway plays or rock concerts to attend. You could find activities when you aren't doing chores for survival. There would be no barber shops or beauty parlors to get your hair done. Booze would be plentiful as it gets better with age. If you want fresh fruits and vegetables you can plant a garden for this. That's another chore to take up some of your time. It would be best if you took up a new house on the outskirts of town where there is plenty of land for animals and a garden. You could find a farm near most large cities. Now you're a farmer not by choice as much as by necessity. This would make survival easier for you and your family. When the children get older they could help out with the chores. In the sunbelt you could have a garden year round if it doesn't get hurt by frost. You would plant one after another and hope for the best. If you knew when the weather was going to turn cold, you could cover the garden up with hay or straw. It might be a good idea to do this in the winter months as there would be no weather reports on the T.V. It wouldn't be all bad, but if you think about it, we've got it pretty good the way it is now. I wouldn't want to change it.

Chapter 15

OUR CHANGING TIMES

We live in a world of change. Everything changes at one time or another. I got my first idea that things change when I was very young. A friend of mine set out to prove this point to me. He said that everything changes; the world is never the same. If you threw a piece of paper on the ground you would change the world. If you picked it up it would be the same I said. He said no because before you picked it up it was on the ground and you changed the world again. It's a very simple principle to understand in this manner. There are all kinds of changes in the world today as there has been for centuries. We live in a changing world. I once heard someone say that "Every time I figure out the game, they change the rules on me." We have to get used to a life of change. There could be no progress without change. If we didn't have change, we'd still be living like cavemen and women. Life has attained a good quality because of change. We no longer see a physician who puts leaches on our skin to effect a cure for our diseases or does blood letting to cure us. Modern medicine is miraculous to behold. Transportation is not limited to feet anymore. We have the automobile and other means of transportation. Food isn't limited to a part of a wild beast cooked over an open fire. Water supplies are more sophisticated than a stream or river. In general, the quality of life is much better overall. This is due to change.

Some things are more constant and we tend to hang on to these from a fear of change. You can always see the sun rise in the east and set in the west. There are 365 days in the year except leap year. This is a minor change that only happens every four years. It's not too much to get used to. When you see dark clouds in the sky you expect rain and usually get it. When you flip a light switch you expect to see light and usually do. When you turn on the faucet, you expect to get water from the tap and it almost never fails to come out. The history of the world is always the same year after year. The new events that take place are history in the making. When you watch the news on T.V., you're witnessing history. Future generations will read or study about the first man on the moon and we saw it happen in our lifetime. Many other events that happen in your lifetime will become history for your children to read about. Encyclopedia companies make year books to update the set on your bookshelf. The outstanding events of the past year are listed in these books. We need to get used to change in everyday life. It's a part of living. If you feel like they changed the rules all you have to do is learn the new ones and you'll be O.K. It's truly a world of change that we live in.

Chapter 16

RELIGION

One form or another form of religion has been around since the beginning of time. Every religion has a Deity or God. Someone or something to worship. One culture worshipped the sun. The Romans had many gods to pray to and believe in. Today most religions have one Deity or God. The laws of God as listed in the Bible are not the only laws that many churches would have you obey. They have man made laws to guide you as well as the laws of the Lord. Attending services on a regular basis is a good habit. It will add strength to your character. It can be very inspirational. It's a time set aside for you to communicate with God or whoever your Deity is. One religion worships Budda as their Deity.

I have my own beliefs about going to service. I haven't been in years and I'm not proud or ashamed of it. It's just the way that I feel about church services. I was brought up Catholic and attended church six days a week for eight years and I figure that's enough church to last a lifetime. I'm not saying that you should stop going to church just because I don't. If you feel good about it, then by all means keep going. I just never felt as close to God during services as when I was in the church alone. It was dark a bit and the candles glowed to my satisfaction. I felt one with God. The church was open all day and night in those days. Today they lock them up so that you can't go in. It's to prevent crime I'm sure, but it keeps out the honest people who want to pray in isolation or with only a few others. If you're lucky enough to have your church open to accommodate you than by all means go in and pray. Just you and God all alone in the church. There's nothing quite like it. I hope you get this experience if you haven't already.

We learn from religion in one way or another. It may be your priest or minister who teaches you your most valuable lessons or it may be a layman. It was a layman who taught me the following. In keeping with positive thinking we look to the lessons in the Bible for inspiration. There's one place where it says "Ask and you will receive; Seek and you shall find; Knock and it shall be opened to you". You can find this in the Bible if you look. I know it's in there, but not just where. It just shows you that positive thinking has been around for a long time. If there's one book that you can absolutely trust in, surely it's in the Bible. Just remember that one-liners are misleading sometimes. I've said before that you have to start small with your goals and build up to the bigger ones. You have to temper your ambitions with a bit of moderation. This principle will work, but you must start small with your goals. Teach your children about religion. Everyone should be informed.

Chapter 17

BRAINSTORMING

Brainstorming is what they do in big business. Other people may do it too. You can get together with family or friends and do it. No doubt you've seen a board meeting on T.V. or in the movies. There's someone at the head of the table like the president of the company or the chairman of the board who leads the meeting. They are usually the bullish dictator type. They speak and the yes men or women say yes sir. This isn't the way that brainstorming works at all. It's more democratic. Everyone has a chance to speak. The idea is to stimulate an idea in the minds of the other members present. To work out an idea or two or more so that all can benefit from it. You remember the old saying that two heads are better than one then it stands to reason that three or more heads are better than two. When one person presents an idea it stimulates the thinking of the others and many times a real gem of an idea emerges from the session. If you've ever had a problem and discussed it with a friend or family member they probably sned some new light on the matter for you. If you can get good results from just one person just think how good it could be if there were more than one other person involved. You may not realize the full potential of brainstorming now but if you try it with others, you should get a better idea of how it words. Once a friend and I were in the screen printing business in St. Louis and we went our separate ways. Well, I was left on my own to do what I could to make the business work for me. I knew how well the Arkansas Razorbacks did in football and how popular they were with the folks in Arkansas. Since we had lived there, I had a check book from the bank where I had done my checking and it had a picture of the Razorback hog on it. This was all I needed to get a silk screen made. I took the picture to my screen maker and the next day he had the screen ready. I took it home to the basement and began printing sweatshirts with it. I made quite a few and also some cheer chiefs out of handkerchiefs. They had the picture on them and not counting my time to print them and the little material used, they only cost a dime each. I sold them for a dollar each for a nice profit. I made a trip to Newport, Arkansas and stopped several places along the way to sell wares. When I had gotten there and used up all of the places that I could think of to sell the merchandise I stopped by my father's house nearby. We talked over what I had been doing and he suggested that I offer the rest of the merchandise to a local merchant at the local mall in town. If he was willing to take all of the merchandise I could give him a discount and that would make the deal more attractive to him. Well, my father was right. He took all of what I had left. That's just one example of how brainstorming can work for you. Try it; you'll like it.

Chapter 18

PICKING A MATE

You may feel that this is an easy task. Just pick out someone you like and you're set. All too often using this logic it ends badly. Picking your mate is one of your three major purchases so to speak. There's your house, your car and your mate. You should give a lot of consideration to each of these purchases. A wrong decision could set you back years on any of these. I just traded in my Cadillac on a New Mercury. I had paid $15,000.00 for the Cadillac and after two years, I got $4,000.00 trade in for the Cadillac. I took a beating for sure. The car was a Diesel and they lost their value very rapidly. If I had picked a car objectively and found out about how bad the re-sale value was on diesels I could have avoided the hardship. My apartment has depreciated since a year ago. Property in general is down and you couldn't do much about it. There were warnings that the market would go down and if one would have listened to these warnings and waited for the market to go down one could have gotten a better buy on property. We have to pay the consequences of our actions whether they be good or bad we have to pay. It's the same with a mate. If your mate sweeps you off your feet with their charm you may be disappointed later. You should do all that you can to find out what kind of person they are before you get too much involved. It seems that more times than not many of us have made bad choices in a mate. Much to our regret, we find out too late. So maybe you agree that we should pick a mate carefully. How do we go about doing this? Well, the first thing that you want to find out is what kind of personality they have. Are they the kind of person who will give you a hard time when you break up if you do break up. Of course you want the relationship to last forever, but more than half of the marriages in this country end in divorce. A lot of us end up married more than once. From a woman's point of view you will want a dependable man who will pay you child support when the marriage breaks up so that you can get by in life with the added burden of children and the added expense they incur. From the man's point of view, you don't want a woman who is vindictive and wants to take you to the cleaners when the divorce goes to court. My friend lost his house to his wife and she even wanted to take his car when she had a car of her own. My first wife wasn't present at our divorce so it was much on my own terms. There was an allowance for child support and she lost the house because she nor I could make the payments. My second wife got the divorce when I was out of town and asked for nothing. My third wife made the terms of my last divorce. She asked for a liberal amount of child support and half ownership of our house where she lives now. She owns half of the house, but she lives in it with my last two kids, Vickie and Michael.

I haven't done badly for three divorces. The last one also gets automatic cost of living increases in her child support. I feel it my responsibility to pay for the support of my children, so it's no big deal. The only hardship at present is that we live in a small two bedroom apartment which is going up for sale so that we can get my step children to live with us until they go to college in two and three years. I get along well with my present wife. We don't argue, but rather discuss matters of importance calmly. We're compatible by horoscope too. One way that I found out about how she was was to loan her money. She always paid it back as she said she would. This shows that she has character. There are other things that you can do to test your prospective mate. Do they tell stories about other people that are untrue? This is bad. Do they go to work every day unless they are sick? Are they dependable? Besides testing for character you can be sure that you two are compatible signs in your horoscope. It couldn't hurt. You could also make a list of the major things that you want in a mate and check them off. If you find someone that you are strongly attracted to and they get about 80 percent on your checklist that isn't bad. Things like color of hair are easy enough to live with if you prefer a blonde and you get a brunette it isn't so bad at least in my opinion. Make a list of the features you want in a mate and if you get about 80 percent consider, yourself lucky. You can list all sorts of things on your list. Personality and earning ability, cooking ability, cleanliness, habits and so on. If the list you make reflects your true feelings for the qualities you want in a mate then don't settle for too much less or you won't be happy in the future. The two of you should have similar interests in life. If you both like going to a movie it will be easy to spend time together where you both enjoy yourself. The more things that you both like doing together the better off you will be. Let's hope that you and your mate go through your golden years together. But just in case it doesn't work out, let's hope that you don't get burned after the divorce. There are a lot of men who don't pay what they are supposed to pay for child support or alimony. This can be a big hardship for the woman who's left to bring up the children. Loosing your house and car and your savings account is no fun for the man either. Pick your mate carefully. Take it from one who has had lots of experience in picking mates. Do yourself a favor and choose carefully. If you are on your second or third or latter mate and you break up you should be aware that we tend to attract the exact same kind of person that we had before. You have to be careful to avoid this if you had a bad mate previously. If you had a good mate it will be easy to attract the same type of person. Just remember to be choosy the next time you pick a mate.

Chapter 19

CHRISTMAS IN JULY

Usually the stores put out the Christmas stuff early but not as early as July. What's it all about this Christmas in July? Well, it's one way to get ahead of the game. You can start looking for presents in July. Sometimes if you wait until the last minute you may not have a very big selection and you may have to pay top dollar for what you want. The crowds at the stores get bigger and sometimes people fight over one item that they both want and there is only one left. It takes forever to get through that checkout line during this busy time of year. You can save yourself a lot of aggravation by shopping early. All stores have sales the year round and if you start looking in July you could be finished way ahead of December 24th or 25th. You could be all through in November. Then you could sit back and laugh at the poor people caught up in the huge crowds doing their shopping at the last minute. It's a good idea to start saving for the next Christmas right after the last one in over three months you'll have a nice amount put aside for the upcoming holiday and can get started early. Go shopping more often and pick up what you need for everyday and don't fail to look the merchandise over thoroughly. You're looking for super bargains. I've found $40.00 toys on sale for as little as

$5.00. This is a must purchase item if you need a toy for a son or nephew or whomever. All year long there are bargains galore from one time to the next. You have to be there to take advantage of these bargains. Be an alert shopper and learn to spot the bargains. If it's over 50 percent off, it's a bargain and you'll want to pick it up if you can use it as a gift for someone on your list. If you're at a store and you spot a bargain go ahead and buy it and if the purchase runs you a little short on cash, you can get the money back out of your Christmas savings. You can put these early purchases on a closet shelf and wait till it's near time to wrap them or you can wrap them as you get them. Either way will work fine just choose the one that suits you best. You're going to like Christmas in July. It will save you both time and money and eliminate the hustle and bustle of the busy holiday. If you like getting caught up in the crowds and being a part of the Christmas spirit you can always go out to a busy store and be a part of the season. Since your shopping is finished, it's your choice as to whether you want to pick up something and get in the busy line at the cash register or avoid it entirely. I get my shopping done early and then go out and mix in with the holiday crowds. I like to get caught up in the spirit of it all. There's usually a little old man or lady with a bell and a kettle collecting donations for some charity. Mixing with the crowd and knowing you don't have to buy anything or stand in line is a nice feeling. Try it this year and see how well you like it.

Chapter 20

CREDIT CARDS

Those little rectangular pieces of plastic, how wonderful or disastrous they can be. We live in an age of credit and it's a good thing that we do. Who could buy a house without credit? What about a car? Then there's major purchases when we're short on cash. A credit card or credit in general can be your best friend. It makes it easy to get on with the business of living. No money down and a little each month. It's a way of life. It's best to use your credit wisely. If you don't you can bury yourself in debt and never get out. Some loan companies have the same customers for years and years. They never get out of debt. You have to know how to handle credit so that it doesn't get the best of you. My wife is a poor manager of credit. She had a checking account and was always bouncing her checks. In a short time, she had paid out a considerable amount in fees for bad checks. She had to close her checking account because she couldn't manage it properly. I gave her my Amoco credit card to use in an emergency if she needed a repair. She charged gas on it and ran the bill up so high she had trouble making the payments. I took the card away from her. If she'd have kept it for another month she'd have been in real financial trouble and messed up my credit with that company. Another friend of mine had a checking account and when he got a letter from the bank, I went in with him to straighten it out. When I looked at his record of checks there were only a few listed. He had the idea that when he needed money all he had to do was write a check. He had to close his account also. If you don't manage your financial affairs properly you can get in over your head. One wise thing to do with your major credit card is to charge Christmas purchases. Well let me explain; you should have some money in a savings account at a savings and loan that pays interest from the date of deposit to the date of withdrawal. You can then charge something when you see it on sale at a good price and when the bill comes in go to the savings and loan and take out enough money to pay the bill. Don't charge more than you have money to pay for. Know where the money is coming from to pay for your charges. Don't go overboard. It's easy to do. You get the idea that it's free. You pick out what you want and just give the cashier your credit card. All the money you had when you went in the store is still yours to keep. You got something free. Well, we all know that this isn't true. Soon the bills come in and you wonder how you spent so much money. Don't be foolish with your credit. Whether it is in one form or another, if used properly, credit can be a wonderful thing. Use some common sense when it comes to credit. Don't buy more than you can pay for when the bills come in. I've never known any of my bills to be misplaced. They all come in regularly.

Chapter 21

INVESTMENTS

There are many investments you can make. The more money you invest, the more you stand to make. First I think it's wise that you set up a savings account with from $1,000.00 to $5,000.00 in it for minor emergencies. This should be readily accessible to you. The money is there for an emergency and most emergencies don't wait very long to get settled. An ordinary passbook account at a bank or savings and loan will be adequate for this purpose. I prefer a savings and loan for several reasons. Most of them that I've come in contact with pay interest from the date of deposit to the date of withdrawal. Many banks pay quarterly so that if you take the money out one day or more before the quarter ends you lose the interest for nearly 90 days. This money will be in a low interest account because it is readily available. You're not trying to make money on this money, it's there for an emergency. Savings and loans do pay a little more interest to my knowledge. Even the same as the bank would be O.K. It would be more interest even if the rate was the same if you took some of it out near a quarter date. You may prefer a bank and it's O.K. as the real dollar amount of interest on this amount of money isn't much in the first place. Now that you have got emergency money you can use the excess cash that you have for investments. There are many kinds of investments and I recommend that you seek the advice of an expert in the field. Seek the advice of several or more experts. Of course a bank officer can tell you of all of the benefits of certificates of deposit paying 8 or 10 percent maybe better. That's about all he can offer you. An investment firm has a lot more options for you to consider and some of them are at a much better rate than a certificate. Look over many investments and find one or more that are right for you. A nice lady at a local investment firm calls me from time to time to tell me about investments. There's a mutual fund paying about 37 percent that isn't too safe, but there's another mutual fund paying about 33 percent that is safe to invest in. Then there's a tax free municipal bond or more than one paying about 10 percent fully insured and you don't pay taxes on the interest. You've already paid tax on the principal, so there are no taxes. She mentioned that it would depend on what tax bracket a person was in as to which way would be best. I had heard of an 80 percent tax bracket and figured she was right. Just today I asked a lawyer who comes in the coffee shop where I hang out about the limit on taxes. He said that there used to be a 80 percent bracket, but President Eisenhower did away with it and made the limit 50 percent. That was the best news I've had in a long time. Now when I look at the two investments that I like, it seems that even if you were in a 50 percent tax bracket, you would still net more from the mutual fund paying 33 percent than the municipal bond paying 10 percent tax free. It's simple arithmetic to me. If all of your income is taxed at the rate of 50 percent then so would be the return from the mutual fund be taxed at 50 percent which would net you 16½ which is better than 10 percent. Mutual funds can fluctuate, but a 33 percent one would have to drop a considerable amount to make it a bad deal. If you can find one fairly safe that is paying about 33 percent it would be a good investment. The secret to the safety in a mutual fund is the word mutual. It tells the story. The money in the fund which is yours and mine and everybody's is diversified into many investments so that if a few lose money there are others that can make up the difference to make the fund strong. I put $20.00 a month into a fund that was supposed to double in value over 20 years but after about 8 or 9 years it was still the same so I got out of it. I've learned since then. It's the same story as the banker who can only show you a few investments. The salesman who sold me the fund didn't have much to offer. Now I shop around for the best deal available.

The stock market is another form of investment. Money is made and lost in the stock market. You may feel that it is too risky for you. In general, it's more of a gamble than an investment. There are blue chip stocks that are pretty safe but don't return a lot. The bigger the risk, the bigger the return or loss. I don't know much about penny stocks except that they are cheap to buy and if they take off you can do real good. Seek the advice of a competent financial advisor and make your decisions wisely.

There's another type of investment available where they have dog racing. They have it here and in the next two years, I plan to look into it seriously. You can buy racing dogs and possibly make money off of them. The way I heard the details from a lady who owns dogs here was as follows. You can get a puppy from a litter for about $1,500.00 to $2,000.00 each. Then you can make a deal with a kennel to board him, raise him and train him and race him all at no additional expense out of your pocket. When he starts racing, you collect 35 percent of all the money he wins. If he makes grade A and races in that class you get 50 percent of his winnings. Some have a lot of dogs and some have a few. The numbers for some of them run up pretty high. It doesn't seem like it would be too hard to get your money back and make a nice profit in the deal. If you don't live in or near a town where they race greyhounds, you could take a trip to one and look into buying a dog or more than one if the idea appeals to you.

It's a different story with horses. All of the expenses are yours and aside from a much higher price for one of these animals some of them don't make enough to pay their feed bills. They break their legs more than dogs and have to be put to sleep when this happens. Horses look like a bad investment to me.

You can also invest in commodities. I think that you'd be

crazy to do this because a man who sold commodities for years told me that 95 percent of the people who invest in commodities lose their shirt. It's a high risk investment. Gold is one commodity where you may make out O.K. I'll just pass on the information to you that I know about. There are a couple of sisters who live in California who make predictions. I suppose that they are psychic or whatever. Well, according to the information that I got, they have an accuracy record of 95 or 99 percent. That means that nearly every prediction that they make comes to pass. Ninety-five or 99 out of 100 make the grade. They could be wrong, but according to the information that I got they have a good track record and it could happen. It's up to you if you want to take a chance on it. They predict that gold will go up to over $4,000 per ounce by September 1986. It may or may not, but it isn't likely that gold will ever be worthless. It's been a valuable metal for centuries.

Some people that I've talked to prefer silver to gold, but this is supposition on their part. It's likely that if gold rises, so will silver. Personally, I think silver is good, too. It's a lot cheaper than gold for the investor who doesn't have a big bankroll to invest gold and silver went up a few years back and there were those who made money from it. A friend of mine had $5,000.00 worth of silver and it went up to $50,000.00 He sold it for a nice profit. Silver is another metal that has been around for centuries. Judas received silver for betraying Jesus.

Precious stones such as diamonds are another good investment if you can buy them cheap enough. They advertise one carat diamonds here for about $495.00 I saw an ad on cable T.V. from New York for one carat diamonds for $295. You have to shop around. If you buy from a jeweler, it will take years and years for them to appreciate to what you paid for them. I bought a diamond ring with eight small diamonds and a larger one in the middle. The regular price was $500.00. It was on sale for $250.00 I've asked at different stores how much they'd give me for it and my best offer was $40. For diamonds, the best prices would be at the DEBers sale in Africa if you can get in and then they sell in lots that they have chosen. You can't break up a lot. You either take all or nothing. If you could buy stones in India you may get a good price or the same goes for Columbia. You would have to be set for a large purchase to make all of the travel and trouble worth your while. Beware of companies selling stones in the mail order business. I bought some from one company and they substituted diopside for black stars. None of the stones that I bought were of great quality and some were downright poor. Very poor. Choose your investments carefully and seek advice at every opportunity.

Chapter 22

YOUR PERSONAL BUDGET

Why have a budget? The alternative is to have a dollar drain. If you don't have a budget, you probably really don't know where all of the money goes. I've had a budget for about twenty years now. It helps me keep track of my money. If you think that a budget is a good idea, then read on and I'll show you how to put one together. It's not too hard once you get the hang of it. Since many of our bills come in once a month, we want to get on a monthly basis. If you get paid once a month, this will be easy. It will take a little effort if you get paid bi-weekly or weekly. You can use a spiral notebook to keep monthly records of everything. Start by listing the big bills at the top of the page, work your way down. You can list the bills that come in or are due on the first of the month and the later ones later on your list. In addition to your monthly bills, you have daily or weekly ones. It helps if you put these on a weekly basis all together. I consider gas for the car and meals out and spending money as "Spex". My word for spending and expenses. I allow $100.00 per week for this and list it on my budget as $400.00 per month. I squeeze by on the few extra days. Everything else is monthly. When I run out of cash I write a check to cash and take it to the bank for the green stuff. I budget my weekly money so that it lasts at least a week or more. If I have a lot left over when it's time to write another check sometimes I spend it on a movie or whatever. It's easy to

82

spend excess cash. Even my kids are good at it. It takes little talent to spend money. The trick is to manage it properly so that it does what it is supposed to do. Once you've listed all of your expenses you should list your income and convert it to a monthly amount. It should be more than the total of the bills. If it isn't, you're in trouble. You may have to take another job to supplement the amount of the deficit. Once your income is more than the total of the monthly bills you're in good shape. The excess can be saved or invested.

A spiral notebook has a dividing line in the middle which comes in handy. List each bill on the left side by writing its title and the amount near the dividing line. Once they are all listed, then make two lines down the paper on the right of the divider so that on the right side you will have three columns at the top of the page. On the right side write the date. In the next column, write balance for balance and O.M. for outstanding minimum. You can either do one of three things that I suggest. No. 1. Set up a checking account. No. 2. Use cash and keep it in a safe place. No. 3. Use a savings account to disperse your money for paying the bills and whatever else you use it for. I recommend a checking account. It is easy to keep the cancelled checks if you ever need proof that you paid a bill. Using money orders makes it harder to keep a record of paid bills.

It can be done, but it's troublesome. A checking account is your best bet. At the beginning of the month, after you pay the first of the month bills, put a check mark by the ones that you paid. Then you know they are paid. List your balance in checking or savings or cash on hand. If you get paid weekly, your balance will be different from time to time. Always have a record of your unpaid bills and the amount you still owe for the month. Keep the check list up to date to the day. Now that you've got it on paper, it's easy to see just where you stand at any given time. Use spex in your budget. See how little cash you can get by on in a week. Then you can add a little for the week where you spend a little more and you'll know what it takes you weekly in spending and expenses (spex). Don't forget to take into account any yearly expenses that you have: things like car insurance or real estate taxes, if your house is paid for.

Homeowner's insurance is another yearly expense. If you're making house payments, these last two are probably included in the payment. If your annual insurance is $600.00, you should allow $50.00 a month to pay it when it comes due. The same goes for other yearly expenses. Good luck with your budget.

I am making a copy of my own budget so you can get a better idea of what one looks like.

August 1984

		Date	Bal.	O.M.
House No. 67	269.98	8/1/84	789.00	794
2nd Deed no. 10	258.33	8/4/84	689.00	694
Apt. No. 57	380.02	8/10/84	639.00	644
Add'l Ch. Sup't	47.00			
Car No. 2	185.49			
Mom No. 2	100.00	8/14/84	539.00	544
Cable	39.45	8/18/84	514.00	519
Charges	30.00	etc.	etc.	etc.
Phone	75.00			
Gas	20.00			
Elec.	60.00			
Spex	400.00			
Gro.	50.00			
Visa	50.00			
Ins.	70.00			

$2034.xx

Income: 1547
409
75
10

$2041.00

I've added a few cushions to my budget and advise you to do the same. One bill or another will go higher from time to time so the extra money you allow in your budget is a cusion to allow for these added expenses. In my budget, I made available an extra $30.00 under the heading of charges. Now I use it to add to the $50.00 I've allowed for paying Visa as the bill is higher now. I also have my car insurance paid in full for the next year so I can add this $70.00 to my Visa payment also. Altogether, if I have no unforeseen expenses, I can send Visa $150.00 per month. In August my AAA dues are due, so I'll subtract $51.00 from the Visa payment to pay AAA. My gas bill is usually under $10.00 or so when that bill is paid. I used to allow $50.00 for electric, but with summer coming, I added another $10.00 to make it $60.00. I will now leave it at $60.00 and if it's less I'll have money left over. If it's at all possible, for you to add a few cushions, into your budget, you should by all means do this. It's always better to come up with more money in your account or on hand than it is to come up short. I don't buy much in the line of groceries, but I do buy cigarettes so I allow $50.00 for this. It's more than enough as I only spend about $30.00 on cigarettes each month. This is another cushion so that I don't run out of money before the end of the month. Make a budget. You'll be pleased with the results.

Chapter 23

MENU SHOPPING

Saving money is very good for your budget. It gives you more to spend or save. One way you can cut expenses is by shopping over the menu when you go out to eat. Almost every menu I've looked at offers one or more good values. If you can eat a large variety of food you should be able to find the best value on the menu. Before I go into food I want to mention drinks. This is a high profit item for a restaurant. 50¢ for a cup of coffee is way too much in this day and age. If you consider how many glasses of soda you can get out of a bottle you buy in the supermarket you can see that this is another high priced item. The same goes for just about everything you're offered to drink. Few places offer a good buy on drinks. If you can get by with just water you'll save considerably. For a family of five the drink bill alone could easily run $3.00 plus tax. Even more for breakfast if you get coffee and juice. If you must have a drink with your meal you may get a better value with the larger size. Check this out before you order.

Now for food. We eat out all of the time. We're constantly looking for new and better places to eat. I always look at the menu to spot the values and try and get the best one that I like. A well known chain offers combination plates some are good values and some are not. One of these has a small serving of cottage cheese and a sliced boiled egg and a few tomato slices on a large mostly unedible lettuce leaf. That's all you get for $3.55. Not a good buy at all. I would like to order this once in a while but never do because it is such a rip off. You can figure the value of a food like the one I described from the a la cart menu list. Cottage cheese is about 80¢ and one egg is 60¢ and an order of tomatoes is about 70¢. That adds up to $2.10 not $3.55. You would be overpaying $1.45 for this plate. On the other hand they have a breakfast special for about $2.79 and if you add up the items separately it's a good value. You get two eggs worth about $1.60 and four sausages or bacon strips worth about $1.50 and two pancakes worth about $1.40. That's a $4.50 value for $2.79. A good deal. This meal can be ordered any time of day. Sometimes we eat it for supper. They used to be reasonable on chili but now are ridiculous it's about $2.70 for a bowl of chili. I used to get a bowl of chili and a side order of noodles and make chili mac with the two ingredients. It was cheaper than their beef and noodles but it's no bargain any more so I don't get it. Another restaurant we go to is a family run operation with home cooking. The food is good and plentiful. They have price discrepancies on different foods when you order them as a full meal as opposed to a la carte. Two dinners are 50¢ more for the dinner and one is 70¢ more for the dinner and one is $1.00 more for the dinner. You get the same items with the dinner no matter what you order. In a la carte you get soup with your meal and if you order the dinner you get choice of soup or salad and tea or coffee and jello or ice cream for the extra price you pay. Many people look at the menu only to pick out something that they want to eat with no regard to the price. You should shop every menu that you look at. It can save you a lot of money over the years. Another way to save money when you eat out is to get your hands on some food coupons or discounts. We love to get coupons or discounts on food. We have a coupon book now and use it often. Sometimes you can get two items for the price of one which is a real bargain. Keep an eye out for coupons. They're great money savers. If you can't get some coupons you can still save with the basic idea of menu shopping. Even if you don't eat out often you can get an idea of the different prices for your favorite foods. Prices will vary from one place to the next. Find the best price for each of your favorite foods and then eat at the restaurant with the best price for the food you're hungry for at any given time. Sometimes you've got more cash than you need and feel like a treat so you go to a high priced restaurant for a meal. There's nothing wrong with treating yourself and a friend or mate or sate. Even though you're prepared to spend a lot more for your meal you can still shop the menu. It helps to be good with simple math. Addition, subtraction and multiplication and division. You can break down the price of a steak to price per ounce and then compare the 10 ounce to the 14 ounce and see which one is the better buy. If they are the same price per ounce you can order the small one if you're not too hungry or the large one if you are hungry. One thing you want to keep an eye out for if you like boiled shrimp is all you can eat deals we've found a few, but one chain closed. When you consider a shrimp cocktail with a few shrimp on it is about $4.00 you're really getting your money's worth if you can get boiled shrimp on an all you can eat deal. Here we do have one place where a dinner runs about $10.00 and comes with all the salad you can eat and all the boiled shrimp and all the beer, wine or soda you care to drink. All in all it's a good deal if you want to spend the money. Try different places and find the ones where the best values are so you can go to them when you eat. Shop the menus every time you go to see if you can spot changes to your benefit. If you find that they've raised the price too high you don't have to order the item that's overpriced. This is only one way to save money and fight inflation. There will be more ideas in another chapter.

Chapter 24

SUPERSTITION

Throughout history there has been one superstition or another. You probably know a few yourself. Some people are very superstitious. Even to a ridiculous point. There is some fact and some myth about superstition. Take the one about walking under a ladder. Many times a ladder will have someone on top of it. Many times this someone will have a can of paint or something else that wouldn't be good if it fell on you. When a ladder is leaning up against a building the most likely spot for something to fall is right under it. In the middle of the space between the bottom of the ladder and the wall on which it's leaning against. If you walk under it this is the likely spot where you will walk so that if something falls from up above it is likely to hit you on the head. That's one good reason why you should not walk under a ladder. You may walk under many ladders and not get hit in the head or elsewhere but I avoid them just in case it's my unlucky day. There's the one about three on a match is unlucky. From what I hear about it there were three men taking a light off one match in a foxhole during a war and the light attracted the enemy fire and the third man got shot. It's not likely to ever happen again. When I was younger I've seen buddies of mine blow out a match so that there wouldn't be three on it. Just silly superstition. There are those that are supposed to bring you good luck also. I don't think it hurts to indulge in these even if they don't work. They can add something to a conversation. I carry two four leaf clovers in my wallet and a two dollar bill for good luck. While I had these marvels with me at various events of gambling I've lost many times. Sometimes I've won but I don't give any credit to my luck charms. If a lucky charm was truly lucky you couldn't lose no matter how hard you tried. You could bet the longest odds in a race which don't have a prayer of winning and you would win every time. The only sure thing that I know of is if you're psychic or have E.S.P. and can see into the future ahead of time. I'm working on this all of the time. If you can develop these powers you can get rich in a hurry. You could foresee the future and see the numbers of the winners at the horses or Jai Alai or the dogs or even bingo. The potential is unlimited if you can only develop these powers. Short of having this gift or developing it you will have to take your chances with the majority of the people. I've made it a hobby to try and develop these powers. You can do the same you've got nothing to lose. You may succeed in your efforts and if not, it will give you something to do that will keep you busy.

Chapter 25

YOUR CAREER

I've touched on this subject lightly in another chapter and want to go into more detail now. Some people say that you are what you eat. But I say that you are what you are. If you're a policeman that's what you are no two ways about it. In almost every new conversation you get into the person asks what do you do. What are you in other words. Some jobs have more prestige than others. With the prestige goes more money in most cases. When you look for a career you don't want to be sucked in by a fancy title with minimum benefits. It you're going to have a title you should get good pay to go along with the title. The two main things to consider for your career are ability and preference. You want to be good at what you do but you should be in work that you like. You don't want to be in a job that is a drag and bores you. This will dampen your spirit and likely you'll end up quitting the job. You may have latent talent in one field or another but no training for it. This is O.K. you can always get training in one way or another. I recommend that you find out where your talent lies. You should have potential in more than one field so that you can choose one that you like. For the student in high school or college it will be easy to find out where your talent lies. For the rest of us it will take a little more effort. Don't be discouraged. There is one other thing that you think I left out in considering a career and I'm coming to it now — salary. Your selection should be a harmonious blend of all the factors. A high salary will help you all through your life. The object is to bring in more money than it takes to pay your monthly expenses. This way you have some left over for saving and investing for the future. Everyone should get away from the routine as often as possible. At least once a year. We're going on a trip in two days and you begin to look forward to these things. Here they don't have White Castle hamburgers or Steak "n" sheak hamburgers or two other foods that we like. We're looking forward to the trip. You should do this too. Go on vacation once in a while. It's good to get away from the routine of things. One other thing you should consider in a job are the benefits like paid vacations and hospitilization insurance and retirement funds. Remember the basics of a good job. Be in work that you like and are talented at with good pay and good benefits. That spells a successful lifestyle. Look into what the different jobs pay where you have the talent to do the job. Pick one with good pay and that you like. Remember you'll probably be doing the job for twenty or thirty years before you retire.

Chapter 26

YOUR FUTURE

Begin now to plan for the future. Many people wait until it's too late and can do little to change the inevitible. They think that they will use their social security to have a nice retirement life. When they get near retirement age they check into it much to their disappointment. It doesn't pay that much. Most people on S.S. are struggling to get by. Don't wait until the last minute if you wait and depend on S.S. you may have to take another job to supplement your retirement income. I know of one lady who gets a pension from her old job and a larger amount of S.S. since her husband died and is still working part time to supplement her income. Since her house is paid for she could just get by on what she gets monthly. This lady and her husband never made big money from their jobs but worked together and just before her husband died they finished paying off their house by making all of the payments. You may not be able to get high paying jobs for one reason or another but you can still have something out of life as so many others do. Your estate will grow in direct proportion with your career. If two people work and one makes $5 00 per hour all of his life and the other one makes $10.00 and their spending habits are the same and inflation subsides the one making $10.00 per hour will end up with at least twice as much as the other guy. It's simple arithmetic. I've already gone over career, but want to say that you should strive for a job that will pay well throughout your working life. The more you make the better you can do if you manage your money well. Count on the sure things for retirement. Even if your company has a good retirement plan you may get fired right before retirement so 'they can cheat you out of your benefits. This happens all too often. You may be able to count on your social security and what ever you've saved or invested. If you do get your retirement benefits from the company where you worked for all those years, that's fine but don't count on it for those trips to Europe and places that take a lot of money to vacation at. Learn to depend on the sure things in life. If you have $50,000.00 in a safe investment that's paying you 10% interest you can depend on an extra income of about $5,000.00 per year. The sooner you start doing something towards your retirement the better. It's doubly smart because you can have the best of two worlds if you begin now. Say you've finally managed to put $50,000.00 away for retirement. It's taken a while but now you have it put away. You have several options now. You could take all of the interest and go on a few vacations every year or you could take half of the interest and leave the other half to make your retirement account grow even faster or you could leave it all to build up for retirement. One other thing that you will want to do by the time you retire is to reduce your expenses. Say you start out at age 35 with your final home or apartment. Today 30 year mortgages are offered on property so that by the time you're 65 and ready to retire, you will have paid off the mortgage to reduce your expenses. You'll still have to pay taxes and insurance, but this is far less than the entire payment used to be. By this age you should have enough money to buy several cars to last the rest of your life in a regular savings account. This will further reduce your expenses if you've taken care of the two major expenses that people have in their lifetime. A married couple who both worked for the last five or ten years before retirement will each collect a S.S. check. Assume the man's check is $500.00 and the woman's check is $400.00 per month. That's not bad to retire on today. If the company cheated you out of your retirement benefits this is all you'll have to live on unless you planned ahead for retirement and have an investment or savings to collect interest from. This little extra can make a big difference in your lifestyle. You want to do as good possible so say that the company where you saved for all those years paid up your retirement benefits. Now our couple has $900.00 per month from S.S. and ? from the company. That's even better. It will allow you to travel more because you have more money to do it with. But think how much better it would be if all of your possible retirement incomes came in for you. You'd have S.S. and the company pension and your own savings or investment. You'd be ready to live high on the hog so to speak. You could make frequent trips to see relatives who are out of town or visit those places where you want to go. You could go to Vegas several times a year and maybe hit it big while you're there. It could happen. You know what the Chinese say "No tickee no landree." If you're not here you don't have a chance. Just to show you how close you can come I'll tell you what happened to me on my last trip to Vegas. I played a slot machine with a progressive jackpot at the Golden Nuggett one morning and only put in one dollar at a time. To cash the big jackpot you had to put in three dollars at a time. I hit four Golden Nuggetts for a jackpot of $300.00. Not bad but, if I had put in three dollars on that pull I'd have won $46,000.00 So you see it is possible. The trip was highly enjoyable never the less. We did come home winners. Gambling may not be for you, but there are many other pastimes that you can get involved in; a lot of them take money to do so plan for the future now. I don't want you to get the wrong idea. I believe in living and enjoying life as you go along so spend a little now to enjoy life along the way and save some for the future also. This way you can have the best of both worlds. Don't deny yourself a few of life's pleasures so that you end up saving every penny and die before you get to enjoy what you've saved and your heirs get it all.

Chapter 27

MONEY SAVERS

No matter how much money you make, it's what you've got to show for it that counts. If you take two people with the exact same income and one is a bit of a spendthrift and the other watches how he spends his money the thrifty one will end up with more to show for his money than the spendthrift. This chapter will give you some ideas on how to make your money go farther. This will be a plus to any budget.

Coupons: There are many ways to get coupons and they offer savings on items that you use everyday. There's a woman who is known as the coupon queen. She pays practically nothing for a large amount of groceries when she shops. You may not get this far with coupons but you can save a considerable amount by using coupons than the other editions and make it a point to buy the one with the most coupons in it. This will give you a better selection of items to make a choice from. Find out which magazines offer the best coupons and buy them. If you can get a coupon book for meals and you eat out from time to time this would be a great help with these costs. Some coupon books have a large variety of things at a discount and are a good value.

Your Car: Take care of your car and it will take care of you. Do the necessary maintenance on the car so it doesn't get bad and cost ten times more to fix. You should change the oil and filters at regular intervals. A complete tune up periodically is a good idea to save gas and wear and tear on the engine. You should check the tires for proper inflation to save wear and get better gas mileage out of the car. Keeping it clean will help you get more money out of it when you trade it in or sell it.

Rebates: This is another way to save money. If you can wait to buy an item until you see it has a rebate, you'll save money with this technique. It takes a little effort on your part to mail in the proper label or whatever they require you to send in as proof of purchase so you qualify for the rebate.

Discounts: Do I love a discount or sale on an item that I want to buy? We just got a new microwave about two months ago. I was at the store and decided to take a look at them just to see how much they were. A nice one was on sale because it was the last one in stock. It was marked down $70.00 so I grabbed it and took it home. It's another way to buy what you need and make your money go further. Always try to buy it at a discount. Be a shopper and spend as much time in your favorite store as you can and keep your eye on the items that you want to buy and when they are rediscounted, then go ahead and buy them.

Increment language: Ever notice how many prices end with the two digits 99? There's a reason for this. It's to deceive you into thinking that the item is cheaper than it really is. For example you see a dress or shirt marked $6.99 and right away you say to your friend look at this one only $6.00. Well it's not $6.00 it's $6.99 or to state it better it's $7.00. If you give the cashier $7.00 you're only going to get back a penny if there's no tax. Most of us don't have a keen mathematical mind so the people who are responsible for marketing are always thinking up new ways to fool us into thinking their product is really cheaper than it really is. 99 is easy to translate to the next dollar so they sometimes use prices ending like 79 or 89 or even 69. If the item is worth about a dollar, they'll take whatever little extra they can get so an item might be $1.19 or $1.29 so they can get an extra little change. You'll likely call it a dollar item and not notice the little difference. If you find out the true price when checking out you'll probably go ahead and buy the items anyhow. Learn these tricks of pricing and be aware of just how much an item costs before you buy it. If it's $199.99 the real price is $200.00. You see this increment language makes an item sound cheaper than it really is. If the item is some dollars and more than 50¢ extra then say to yourself the next higher dollar amount so that you get the true picture of the price. Make this a habit whenever you go shopping. Say the item is $8.69. Then say to yourself $9.00 is the cost. In most cases there will be tax and the item will run over the next dollar amount. $5.99 with a 5% sales tax would cost you for the one item $6.29. Look for these pricing gimmicks in the future and know the true price you will have to pay for the items you want.

Bank Accounts: No matter what type you have you will get more interest if you leave the principal in longer. One good way to do this at Christmas time. You can charge all of your gifts and when the bills come in about a month later you can take out enough to pay the bills. You will have gotten an extra month's interest by doing it this way. This is an especially good idea for major purchases.

Long Distance: Rather than run up your long distance phone bills send a letter whenever possible. A stamp will almost always be a lot cheaper than a phone call. Especially if you have a lot to say. I don't say to cut out all calls but one or two a month would add up to a nice savings. My phone bills run over $50.00 every month. I even limit them somewhat to cut the expenses.

Transportation: You may be able to save considerably by taking public transportation or getting involved in a car pool to go to work. You'll save wear and tear on the car and some money as well.

Groceries: Don't go grocery shopping on an empty stomach.

Many people do and end up with more groceries than they wanted and they're still hungry when they leave the store. The hungries can make you an impulsive buyer. This is bad for your budget. Always eat within a few hours of going to the store so your hunger pains don't make you an impulsive buyer who ends up with a large bill needlessly.

Menu: Work up a weekly or monthly menu stressing economy. Shop for the items on the menu by making a list. Stick to the list items only. Pick up other items only if you forgot to list them and have to have them. Toilet paper is a typical item that you could forget and have to have if you out or low. This will help keep down impulsive buying of those things you don't really need to have.

Bulk: Buy in bulk when the price is right. Storage space and perishable items should be taken into consideration. Example: 200 gallons of gas at a 20ᶜ savings wouldn't be a wise buy, unless you own a fleet of vehicles. Learn to compare prices from size to size. This will be a big help in determining which size is the better buy. You should take into consideration if you will be able to use the bigger size before some of it spoils. Sometimes the smaller size is more convenient. Learn to break a price down to price per ounce for comparison of different sizes. Some things don't need it like meat that's $2.99 a pound is the same no matter what the size. One package may be more than another because it has more meat in it. You can save a little by buying the smaller size and won't notice it when you eat the meat. There's very little difference in a pound of hamburger or 18 ounces. (one pound is 16 ounces). Items that come by the gallon and half gallon and quart are just reduced in volume by half on each lesser size. A gallon is 64 oz. and a half a gallon is 32 oz. and a pint is 16 oz. I have that wrong the gallon is 128 oz. and the half gallon is 64 oz. and the quart is 32 oz. and the pints is 16 oz. I think it's right now. At any rate if a half a gallon is $1.20 and a gallon is less than double the price, the gallon is the better buy. You can make a few exceptions for a favorite item that costs more than another one like it if the quality or taste is different. We always get the gourmet small peas and pay more for them. They're nothing like the other ones.

Shopping Rules: Follow these four steps. Know what you are going to buy 2; Get in 3; get it 4; get out. If you like to go shopping for the fun of it leave most of your cash and all of your credit cards at home. Consider the things that you want to buy. If they are really necessary go back with the cash and get them. If not, you've saved money by doing it this way.

Off season bargains: Consider Christmas decorations for half price the day after Christmas; buy and save for next year. Lawn mowers at the end of summer. Winter clothes at the end of winter. Shorts and summer clothes at the end of summer. You can buy the kids' clothes for school early and save. Put them up until school starts and they'll have a new wardrobe for the school year. Any off season items can be a good buy. Another thing you can do is declare your own date to celebrate a holiday like Easter for instance. The next day almost everything related to Easter is on sale at half price. Even if you buy some things before the holiday and pay full price you can buy more after the holiday. Valentines candy can be had for half price the day after. It tastes the same the next day.

Meats: Get to know the butchers in your area. Ask them questions. Learn how meat is marked and labeled to be a wiser buyer. The same cuts of meats can be called by different names at a different store. Example: Kansas City ribs are called Country ribs. Rib eye steaks are sold for one price with the bone and another price without the bone. Look into these types of meat and determine which is the better buy. The butcher can help you with this. If you want to do it yourself you can buy two steaks, one with the bone in and one without the bone. After you eat the steak, weigh the bone to determine how much is wasted. This will help you be a better buyer.

Cases: Buy by the case if savings are there. A store may sell an individual item for 50¢ and a case of twenty four for $12.00.

The price is the same if you buy one or twenty four so if you don't want to lug a case, then just buy a can or more at one time. If you could get the case for $10.00 then it would be worth your while   to get a case. Look for these bargains and make it a habit to buy in quantity all the time when the savings are there.

Banks and Savings and loans: As equally important as the highest rate of interest, are the terms of the account. Some places offer the terms that your money earns interest from "the date of deposit through the date of withdrawal". If you need some money from your savings for an emergency or a vacation or whatever reason, you get full interest from the day you put the money in through the day you take it out. The most common other way is quarterly interest. This pays like on March 31 and June 30th and September 30th and December 1st. If you have an account like this you will lose whatever interest is due you if you make a withdrawal before one of the due dates. Using these dates, you could take out $500.00 on June 29th and loose the interest on that $500.00 for a whole quarter. ¼ of a years interest would be lost.

Christmas Savings: Some banks offer a Christmas savings club. Look into the details of these clubs. Some give you convenient coupons so that it's easy to make a deposit. You may find that these accounts pay no interest at all. Not a good deal for you. I offer you two alternatives to make money off your savings: Open an account at a local bank or S.&L. Pay in x amount of dollars each payday as you would in a club account. Charge your Christmas purchases in December up to the amount you have saved. You will get your most interest on December 31st if it's paid by quarters and the most if it's paid day to day. When the charges come due in January, take out enough to pay them in full. You will avoid paying interest on the charges and can leave a little of your interest in your account and have a head start on the next year. If you prefer to pay with cash, be sure to put your money in an account that pays from date of deposit to the date of withdrawal.

Money management: Keep only enough money on hand for weekly expenses even if you are paid bi-weekly or monthly. You can always cash a check for unexpected expenses like the doctor or a car repair.

W-2's: Don't have your employer overhold your taxes. Save the extra pay you get so that you get the interest for a year rather than letting the government use your money tax free and interest free for you. This will give you more income because of the extra interest you will get from a saving account. When tax time comes you can use the extra money as you would a tax-refund. There will be more of it because of the interest.

Fresh foods: Ready to eat foods cost you extra food dollars. Take a pound bag of french fries at 79¢ and compare to a five pound bag of fresh potatoes at 79¢. You're paying five times the price for ready made. Let this example trigger your thinking for other savings, like the master mind principle.

Furniture: If you are going to make a furniture purchase in the near future why not check the newspaper for a good deal. People relocating in a hurry often have to give their furniture away to facilitate the move. Many times this is expensive furniture at a fraction of the original price.

Vacation: Kids driving you bananas? Try a mini vacation over the weekend. It's definitely cheaper than two weeks cross country and will do you a lot of good. You can take several of these mini-vacations for less than one big one.

Family Finance: Build up a special savings account. When you need or want extra cash you can borrow from the account and pay it back like any other loan. You'll earn interest on the money and save interest charges on the money that you borrow from yourself.

Savings: If you have an excess in savings you can put some to better use by investing it at a higher rate of return. Usually these investments tie your money up so only use the right amount for this purpose. Keep some in reserve.

Insurance premiums: Pay your insurance premiums yearly if you can. There is sometimes a discount for doing it this way. You can also save finance charges when you pay yearly rather than semi-annually or monthly or even quarterly.

Bills: Check into all bills to see if they could be lowered if paid by the year. Some won't be any cheaper, but you may find a couple and save again by doing it once a year.

Charges: Buying with cash is a good policy, but if you have to buy with a credit card or on time then be sure to pay the bill in full when it comes due. This will save you money and that's the name of the game.

Interest: In my opinion, interest rates in some states bear out the term legal piracy. If you buy on credit and add to the total the interest you could say that you gave yourself a cut in pay. That's about what it amounts to. You could pay up to 50% extra maybe more for credit. This can eat up your income in a hurry. Buy with cash if at all possible.

Prescriptions: Ask your doctor to prescribe your medicine by it's generic name if possible. This trick will help you save even more and if you take a lot of medicine the savings add up to a nice amount.

Food: Recently they've come out with generic food. It's been my experience that besides being cheaper it's good food in most cases. If you haven't tried the plain wrappers, you should do it. It's a good value and the food is generally good in quality.

Canned milk: If a recipe calls for milk you can used canned milk for less money and not notice the difference. Powdered milk is another item to consider using in a recipe.

Disposables: Cut out disposables whenever possible. These items just add expense to your budget. Paper items are the worst in my opinion.

Combination: When you set out to do your weekly chores try to combine them. If you make one trip to each of three or four places at different times you will be using excessive gas in your car. If you combine the trips you can save gas. Stop here and then there and so on until you've done all your stops in one trip.

www.ingramcontent.com/pod-product-compliance
Lightning Source LLC
LaVergne TN
LVHW021404080426
835508LV00020B/2446